To Kill an Eagle

Indian Views on The Last Days of Crazy Horse

Edward Kadlecek and Mabell Kadlecek

Johnson Books: Boulder

Fifth Printing 1993

ISBN 0-933472-54-4

LC Catalog Card No.: 81-81580

Cover design: Molly Gough, based on drawings by Amos
Bad Heart Bull

Maps: Llyn French

Printed in the United States of America by

Johnson Publishing Company
1880 South 57th Court
Boulder, Colorado 80301

CONTENTS

PREFACE

This book about the life of War Chief Crazy Horse came about because a number of elderly Indian people told us that certain aspects of the commonly accepted story of Crazy Horse's last days are incorrect or incomplete. They wanted their versions written down and preserved in print, if possible, before they were lost forever.

The second part of *To Kill an Eagle* consists of these old people's stories, which they hoped will stand as their bequest to present and future generations.

The first, less important, part is our own attempt to provide a background for the statements and to synthesize some of the information about Crazy Horse scattered throughout them. It in no way pretends to be a definitive work about the great warrior and his people and should be considered as subordinate to the statements that follow.

We wish to express our gratitude to the Indian men and women whom we have had the privilege of interviewing and who, because of their memories and stories, are the sole reason for this book's existence. These people are: Thomas American Horse, Joseph Black Elk, John Black Smith, Peter Bordeaux, James Chase In Morning, Henry Crow Dog, Jessie (Romero) Eagle Heart, Charles Fire Thunder, Austin Good Voice Flute, Lawson R. Gregg, Dora High White Man, Julia Hollow Horn Bear, Carl Iron Shell, Frank Kicking Bear, Mathew King, Mary Pacer, George Red Bear, Howard Red Bear, Edgar Red Cloud, Paul Red Star, Alfred Ribman, Stella Swift Bird, Frank White Buffalo Man, Everette White Dress, Joseph White Face, Thomas White Face, and Jerome Wolf Ears.

In addition to these, we want all others who have given us bits of information or explanations to know we appreciate their help.

INTRODUCTION

By Edward Kadlecek

Of the many Beaver creeks in the West, one had special significance for the Lakota people. Called *Capa Wakpala* in their language, its source lay in the Dark Forest of northwestern Nebraska. Among the many Lakotas who camped there were Spotted Tail, the head of the Brulé Lakota; Battiste Good (Brown Cap), the Lakota historian; Chief Fast Thunder, the famous scout, and Crazy Horse, the great war chief. It had been Indian country for generations before them, but in 1877 the U.S. government moved the Indian people out of the area into nearby South Dakota.

At the same time, white homesteaders were moving in and erecting sawmills, stripping the timber to provide lumber for their houses. With them came our parents and grandparents. My wife's father was a blacksmith with a shop near the agency headquarters. She attended the government day school as a child and later taught school herself at Manderson and Pine Ridge, South Dakota. I was born on my father's homestead just east of Beaver Valley on one of the tributaries of Beaver Creek.

I grew up and made my living as a farmer and counted as friends and business acquaintances most of the Indian families in Pine Ridge, just north across the state line. I was the familiar *witka*, or egg man, supplying them with farm produce and occasionally leasing their land or hiring them to work. Not long after my marriage, we moved over the ridge to Beaver Valley.

We lived in the valley many years before our friends at Pine Ridge began telling us of its impressive history. We became increasingly interested, but learning was a slow and indirect process. Our deeper involvement with our Indian friends began when Edgar Red Cloud (great-grandson of the famous Chief Red Cloud) talked to me about work for some of his friends. He asked if people in Louisiana, where we had spent the winters for several years, would be interested in seeing Indian dancers and, if so, would I plan a tour for such a group? I agreed, and with his help and that of Henry Crow Dog of Rosebud, South Dakota, and others from Pine Ridge, I became manager and narrator for troups of Indian dancers as they performed around the country from 1961 to 1964. During this time I was often an invited guest at tribal affairs: tribal presidential and council inaugurations, sun dances, inter-tribal dancing contests, and buffalo feasts. Medicine men invited me to the very sacred and private Yuwipi and Native American Church and carefully explained the services to me.

At one point, one of the dancers needed a buckskin dress, and I went to see Jessie Romero Eagle Heart about making one. In our conversation, the steel bridge on Beaver Creek near our home was mentioned. Jessie said that she knew the place, and that it had once been the camping ground of her grandfather, Chief Fast Thunder, in the times before there were such places as Indian reservations.

In the fall of 1962, Jessie; her sister, Mary Pacer; Thomas American Horse, age 96; and Thomas's nephew, Matthew Eagle Heart, came to visit us at our farm on Beaver Creek. American Horse remembered the creek from his boyhood. He knew of the grassy flat just across the low hill from the creek because his father, Chief American Horse, had kept his camp there, and Thomas had spent some of his early boyhood days there. Our farmhouse now stands on the exact location of his father's lodge.

The others knew the place from stories of their parents and grandparents. Mary Pacer remembered the words of her mother: "In the year of 1923 or 1924, my parents decided to gather wild fruit along Beaver Creek. In those days wild fruit was plentiful in this area, and we made camp there to gather fruit. Mother did not join in picking fruit and walked away from camp to be alone. We heard Mother singing and crying because the place where we camped brought memories of her parents. Mother's father, Chief Fast Thunder, had brought Chief Crazy Horse to this place and then had taken him to Fort Robinson."

The reminiscing of the visitors ceased when we showed American Horse a small red pipe that had been found on the hillside some time ago. Taking it reverently in his hand, he turned it slowly to examine its carvings. He spoke softly, saying it was a sacred pipe, one of those made from Minnesota pipestone. He wanted to be shown exactly where it had been found.

The little pipe found on the hillside.

Downstream from our house is a farm pond behind a small earth dam. At the far end of the dam we struggled through the tangled summer's grass until we found the place. American Horse, his feet on the exact spot where the pipe had been found, attached a new stem to it and tamped it full of tobacco. He lit it, then knelt and prayed in the manner of his forefathers—pointing the pipe first to the Great Spirit, then to each of the four directions, and finally to the earth, asking the Great Spirit to bless his people.

Still holding the little pipe, American Horse seemed lost in the past. After a long silence he spoke in Lakota to the others. Then their memories crowded to the surface as they talked freely of the great leaders of the past. Most of their talk was of Crazy Horse because it was here that he and his band often stopped on cross-country trips to the Platte River. And it was here that he made his last stop.

American Horse and his friends asked how far our property extended along the creek and how far north and south. I took them in the car along the road to show them the boundary fences. Later I realized that they had wanted to make sure that certain landmarks were on our property. Back at the farmhouse, they said they had a story to tell about the happenings in Beaver Valley that had never been completely told. They wanted us to put it into writing so that it would not be lost. They said there were other Indian people still living who could add to the story, for many knew of one old camp on Beaver Creek.

Interpreter David Long Black Cat, George Red Bear, Thomas American Horse, and Edward Kadlecek.

Through David Long Black Cat, we met one of these other old people, Julia Hollow Horn Bear of Rosebud, South Dakota, who had long known family stories about Beaver Creek. In the traditional way of storytelling, Julia's grandfathers had told her of its history. Chief Iron Shell, grandfather of her husband Dan Hollow Horn Bear, had often spoken of Beaver Valley—its sparkling creek, its chalky white walls, and the Beaver Mountains to the west side of the valley that provided warriors with places to fast and pray. He told her that the valley had long been known to the Lakota by another name—the "Chosen Land of Crazy Horse."

Iron Shell's family had lived on Beaver Creek and in 1850 his son, Hollow Horn Bear, Dan's father, was born there. Iron Shell and his Brulé Orphan Band had roamed in the north before and during the 1860s. During this time they had associated with the Miniconjous and the wild Oglalas and had come to know personally of Crazy Horse's love for Beaver Valley. Even though the Oglala chief and his band usually encamped in the north, they made regular visits to Beaver Creek and to the Platte River—the Platte for its hunting and trader's supply of guns and ammunition, and Beaver Creek as a meeting place of religious significance.

Julia's grandfather, Brown Cap (also called Battiste Good—the first Lakota to use a white man's name), had lived on Beaver Creek. He was a historian, one of the keepers of the Lakota Winter Count, a calendar record done in picture writing. From these family histories, Julia became so familiar with Beaver Creek that even though she was an old woman before she ever visited the area, she could describe it just as if she had lived there.

Again that fall, Thomas American Horse came to Beaver Valley, this time with George Red Bear, age 85, and David Long Black Cat, vice-president of the Oglala tribe, who served as an interpreter. Both of these men were from Holy Rosary Mission Flats north of the Pine Ridge. As I drove the car slowly along the winding, tree-lined road that in some places touched old travois trails made by his ancestors, American Horse peered intently through the open window. He breathed deeply of the pine-scented air while his lively eyes darted from side to side. Then his body tensed and his gaunt hand shook as he pointed to the bald white butte extending high above the trees. "Scout Point," he exclaimed, and slipped into

Lakota as he talked excitedly to his friend Red Bear. The car crossed the steel-sided bridge, turned into a field, and rolled to a stop at the far end of the earthen dam.

As we began to walk, American Horse made several puzzled turns but always came back to stare at Scout Point. It stood as imposing as it had when Thomas had played there as a boy. Wistfully, he and Red Bear talked of the many things that had changed in the valley. The man-made dam at the valley fork, where they stood, had once been a huge beaver dam, the largest in the valley. Long ago their people had named this stream *Capa Wakpala* (Beaver Creek) for the many beavers that had inhabited its waters. All of the canyons running into Beaver Creek near here had carried more water than now runs in the main stream.

Red Bear knew about the things of which American Horse spoke. He too had been well acquainted with the valley and its history. He had never actually lived here, having been born about the time his people had left the valley—as far as he could remember he had always lived on Mission Flats—but he had been to Beaver Creek many times with other boys of his age. Cutting across the hills and following the old trails, they would ride their ponies over to the creek long after the government had removed their people from it. The boys were responsible for "Indian scares" along the way, but they themselves had often been scared by the white settlers.

American Horse mentioned that cottonwood trees as wide in diameter as a man could spread his arms used to be scattered up and down the valley floor, along with box elders from which his people took sap to sweeten their food and hackberry, whose berries provided seasoning. Ash and elm trees filled the draws, and thickets of wild plums and chokecherries spread over the banks and pressed tightly to the water. Virgin pine, two to four feet through, covered the bordering mountains so thickly that the Indian people had called this the Dark Forest. Most of the huge trees are gone now; crumbling, pitchy stumps—remnants of the lumberman's saw—are the only evidence of their existence.

(Alfred Ribman of Pine Ridge later gave another reason for the lack of large trees. With the aid of his interpreter, Pete Catches, he explained that many trees had been destroyed before the white man came. Returning raiding parties would signal their victories by setting the countryside ablaze while still as much as twenty-five miles away from camp. The size of the fire indicated the degree of success in the raid. When the fire was observed back at camp, the old men, women, and children ran out to meet the returning warriors. Each band leader followed a different procedure for disposing of the gains. Crazy Horse would always distribute the captured horses and ponies to the needy boys of the camp.)

American Horse walked slowly through the field, looking this way and that, taking in every detail. Suddenly his eyes widened in excitement, and he pointed a trembling cane up the valley to a large American elm. Speaking softly, he said that this was a young tree when he had lived here. He moved to the tree painfully but with the eagerness of the boy he had been when he last saw the tree. Removing his hat, he bowed his head and knelt, his gnarled hands clasped over the head of his cane for support. He prayed earnestly and, struggling to his feet, told his companions, "You stand on sacred ground. This is a burial tree known and revered by my people. Here an important wake was held."

After the visits with American Horse and the others in the fall of 1962, we talked with nearly thirty other elderly Indian people from the Pine Ridge, Rosebud, Standing Rock, and Northern Cheyenne reservations. Each had stories to tell and details to add about the events in Beaver Valley. By their own wishes, the people all signed notarized transcripts of their statements to us because, as they said, it was important that the stories be completely recorded in writing, and this had never been done. Julia Hollow Horn Bear said that it was a good thing to do because her grandchildren would rather watch television than listen to her old tales.

We had the help of four interpreters: Joe Black Elk, a tribal lawyer in Pine Ridge; David Long Black Cat, vice-president of the tribe; Joe White Face, a council member from Porcupine, South Dakota; and Pete Catches, a medicine man from Sioux City Community. They translated the statements of individuals who felt more comfortable speaking in Lakota. These people could all understand English, however, and knew that their stories were recorded as they told them.

We consider ourselves honored and very fortunate to have been entrusted by these old people with the preservation of their stories. In a ceremony at the old Sun Dance grounds in Beaver Valley, medicine men and their helpers—Henry Crow Dog, Leonard Crow Dog, Joe Bear Nose, Matthew Belt, and Chris Eagle Thunder— blessed the manuscript of this book, written to keep our promise to our Lakota friends.

PART I

HISTORY

1

THE EAGLE

Grandfathers and grandmothers still talk about Crazy Horse, the renowned warrior of the Teton Lakotas. They tell how he obtained his powers through the guidance of the Great Spirit and how he was like the eagle soaring high and alone, a symbol of power, courage, and freedom. The eagle was a sacred bird, the messenger from the Great Spirit to the Lakota. And Crazy Horse, through his visions, was a messenger, too.

His father was a well-known medicine man and taught Crazy Horse at an early age to respect the powers of the Great Spirit. The son learned well, and it was soon apparent that he possessed the gift of prophecy through vision. He made little mention of his first vision, for it was not his way to share personal feelings or thoughts with others. But it is known that at fourteen, fasting on a hilltop (later called Scottsbluff) near the Platte River, he received another message, one that was to determine the course of his life. Guided by this vision, he began to take part in battles against Indian enemies and white soldiers.

His best friend and teacher was a man called Hump, or High Breast, a strong man with a huge, well-muscled chest. Hump took the young Crazy Horse under his wing, teaching him many useful skills and making him his companion on raiding expeditions. Always the closest of friends, they nevertheless competed with each other in the disposing of enemies and the taking of scalps.

At that time there were three important kinds of warriors recognized by the Sioux. A young man strove to be a great fighter of battles, a great scout, or a great hunter. Usually a man could master only one of these skills, because of the great strength and endurance each required. Hump and Crazy Horse, however, excelled in all three. Such prowess brought them recognition among the Sioux as two of their greatest warriors.

When Crazy Horse was seventeen, the people honored him with a purification ceremony, declaring that he belonged to the "Deity of the Brave." The young man, with his gifts of power and wisdom, would be a great leader. The enemies of the people—among them, the Shoshone or Snakes, Blackfeet, Crows, Flatheads, Rees, Pawnees, and white men—would learn just how brilliant a warrior and defender of his people he was.

In one of his dreams, or visions, which he had again and again, he saw that he would receive power from the Thunder Gods. From others he learned how to use certain objects so that no harm would come to him in battle. One such object was a stone he carried on his person, a talisman everyone knew was sacred. Such an object was referred to as *Tunkan*, for "Grandfather," a term also used for the Great Spirit.[1] Just before going into battle, Crazy Horse would rub this stone all over his body to protect himself from injury. By touching another with it he could give that person protection also.

The stone was so important that Crazy Horse wished to have it with him at all times. Calling his friends together to witness a special medicine man's feat, he held the round, flat rock about as large as his palm, black and quite smooth, and asked his father for a small stick, one of the kind used to clean the stem of a pipe. Turning and twisting the stick with his fingers, he drilled a hole through the edge of the rock. Through the hole, he threaded a buckskin thong. Asking his father to indicate the place on his body where his heart was located, he placed the thong around his neck and passed it under his left arm, letting the stone rest over his heart, providing a bullet- or arrow-proof shield for it. Before a battle, Crazy Horse would ride up and down in front of the enemy lines moving the stone with each turn so that it always hung between his heart and the enemy.

Crazy Horse had more than one kind of "medicine." Besides the ritual of rubbing himself with his potent stone, he made other ceremonial preparations before going into battle. Occasionally he carried a little medicine bag, which he also fastened around his neck. From the bag he would take a small portion of the dried heart and brain of an eagle mixed with dried wild aster flowers. This mixture he would chew, also using some of it to rub on his body. Sometimes Crazy Horse would apply dirt thrown up by the burrowing blind mole to his horse in lines and streaks—not painting him with the dirt, but passing it over him in a certain way with his hands, touching a little of it to his own hair with the addition of two or three short straws of grass. This would render horse and rider invisible and invulnerable to bullets and arrows. Such was the agility and skill of the mounted warrior Crazy Horse that his enemies no doubt wondered if they were indeed battling with an invisible adversary!

This procedure had been given to Crazy Horse by a man who appeared to him in a vision, a man on horseback riding out of a lake in the vicinity of Rosebud Creek, Montana. The man also advised him not to wear a warbonnet; nor should he continue to tie up the tail of his horse in a knot, as was customary among the Sioux. The horse, he said, needed his tail for balance in jumping streams and to brush away the summer flies.[2] Aside from these practical considerations, the great warrior's horses benefited from his power in other ways; they, too, could do strange and wonderful things. Crazy Horse owned two special mounts, a bay and a sorrel. It was the bay who carried its rider in most of the twenty-two battles in which Crazy Horse was victorious. It was the "top" horse in the country and could outrun any enemy horse. After almost constant running in battle, this pony needed only a quick rest to be ready for new forays. Crazy Horse would ride to the top of the highest hill to let his horse "take the breeze." By the time Crazy Horse blew on his eagle-bone whistle, the signal to renew battle, this amazing animal had not only regained its strength and eagerness but could maintain it for another two days of fighting.

Crazy Horse's weapons consisted of a stone war club and a large knife. When charging into battle, he held his war club aloft, and those enemies caught by the flailing weapon were killed immediately. The victims were then scalped with the large knife and the scalps brought back to camp. At the victory dance which always followed a successful battle, the scalps were hung by the light of the fire in the center area. After Crazy Horse and his fellow warriors had danced until daylight, he burned his scalps.

Crazy Horse led his warriors in many battles, some remembered and some not. Fire Thunder particularly remembered a battle in which he took part, and his son, Charles, remembers hearing the story. "I will tell about one of the wars in which he (my father) and Crazy Horse took part. He told me just exactly how it happened as he was there and knew all about it. He told about Crazy Horse's actions in this war. Some Indian warriors went out and my father and Crazy Horse joined them. Those warriors sent scouts ahead of them. The scouts returned and told them that they must hurry to prepare themselves, for soldiers were approaching. They completed their preparations and met the soldiers.

"The warriors and soldiers took positions on opposite sides of the hill and fought. Crazy Horse went along the soldiers' line three times, but they missed him every time. Finally the soldiers took off—they retreated. The Indian warriors chased them and killed some of their group."

As Crazy Horse's skill and power in battle grew, he was honored in many ways by his people, and so it was inevitable that he should be chosen as one of the four "chief warriors" or "shirt wearers"—the official executives for the tribe.[3] The ceremony that made Crazy Horse a warrior chief was held a month or so after the Treaty of 1868; the site of the ceremony was about forty miles northeast of what is now Lusk, Wyoming. The other three young men selected as the head warriors at the time were Young-Man-Afraid-of-His-Horses, American Horse, and Man That Owns a Sword. The new Warrior Chief Crazy Horse had a difficult role to perform, yet he fulfilled his duties faithfully and well. He had taken his place in the leadership of the tribe. Still the eagle, but now more mature and experienced, he was always looking after the welfare of his people.

2

THE WILDERNESS CAMP OF CRAZY HORSE AND HIS BAND

On their hunting trips around large areas of the Dakotas, Montana, Nebraska, and Wyoming the Lakotas had a number of regular camping places. Beaver Valley was one of the favorites. The site was spread out along the creek under huge cottonwood trees in the midst of plum and chokecherry thickets so dense that only narrow animal trails led through them to the water. Tall pine trees covered the surrounding hills.

When Crazy Horse's band and others came up the valley to camp, they followed the Indian-named natural landmarks. On the east side where the present road crosses at the beginning of the hills is an old trail called Sunset Pass. Next come the Beaver Walls, stained and carved, left by the receding waters of an ancient sea. In places these walls are unscalable for several miles, and they finally end far up the creek in a group of buttes dominated by Scout Point. On the west side of the creek stand three pairs of unusual hills several miles apart. The first are White Buttes, now called Sheridan Gates, then Breast Rocks, and finally, past Scout Point, Beaver Mountain and its twin in a range of hills the Lakotas called the Beaver Mountains.

In the immediate vicinity of Beaver Mountain and Scout Point was the Wilderness Camp. This site extends from the place where the pine trees come down on both sides to the creek (the beginning of the Dark Forest) and up past Beaver Mountain to a travois trail that leads up the mountain to the Vision Quest Pit.

Beaver Walls. (*Alderman Photography, Rushville, Neb.*)

Breast Rocks. (*Alderman Photography, Rushville, Neb.*)

White Gates, now called Sheridan Gates. (*Alderman Photography, Rushville, Neb.*)

A travois trail. (*Alderman Photography, Rushville, Neb.*)

Coming up the valley was a well-used travois trail from the north country. Frank Kicking Bear and John Galligo said there were still signs of at least eight other travois trails converging at the camp ground. A trail skirted each end of the ridge containing Scout Point. At the west end was Rosebud Gate, a pass across the high ridge over to the next valley north. The trail that had started near Fast Thunder's camp by the big beaver dam led up the hillside through the pass and on toward White Clay Creek. On the east end, Rosebud Pass trail followed the hilltops eastward. There were also trails along the backbone ridge of the Beaver Mountains leading in from the Niobrara and Platte Rivers. Branches came down around Beaver Mountain itself, one from the Vision Quest Pit and one to Fast Thunder's camp. Today the trails are only parallel ruts washed deep by a century of rains. On the gentler slopes, straight rows of trees grow where the packed earth of the pony tracks made good seed beds.

The high rock, left center, is Scout Point, overlooking Beaver Valley.

Of the buttes around the camp, Scout Point is the most impressive with its high top and massive base. It is a natural lookout station. From there the scout watched for weather changes and game as well as for signs of enemies far out on the prairies toward the Black Hills and for smoke signals or light flashes from friendly bands.

The scout shelter, carved out of the rock above the valley.

At the base of the next butte to the right is the scout shelter where a man could watch over the camp below and see up and down the valley and yet be protected from the weather. On top of this butte was an eagle trap, a man-made pit with an opening to the side for an entry way and a temporary roof of pine branches. A rabbit or snake was fastened on the top where the eagle could see it. When the eagle flew down to take the bait, the warrior waiting on the inside would catch it by the feet and drag it down inside. There he removed the long tail and wing feathers for his costume. As the eagle was the sacred bird, the warrior was very careful not to injure it.

To the left of Scout Point along the wall is a smaller second butte, and past it a third, even smaller one now hidden by pine trees. These three pinnacles were markers of special importance to the parents of Crazy Horse, as will be seen later.

Frequently when Crazy Horse's band passed through Beaver Valley on their way south to the Platte River to secure guns or ammunition, they stopped to hold religious ceremonies. After a good night's rest, a selected group of warriors went to the ceremonial grounds at the foot of the third pair of markers—Beaver Mountain and its twin. Observing the proper ritual, they built a sweat lodge. Then they gathered wood to heat the rocks containing the living spirit. (When two of the rocks are bumped together, do they not make a sound complaining of the hurt? When struck together on a slant, do they not shower sparks that can be used to start a fire? And they do not break, even when heated in the steamy sweatbath lodge for the Purification Ceremony.)

According to Joe Black Elk, Crazy Horse and several others took part in the Purification Ceremony. Later Crazy Horse ascended to the top of Beaver Mountain where he fasted and prayed four days and four nights as he communed with the Great Spirit. He asked the Great Spirit to unite his soul, mind, and body to serve his people of the Sioux Tribe. Standing there on the hill, he held out his sacred pipe—first straight upward toward the Great Spirit above, then outward to the east where the light comes, toward the south where comes the warmth, toward the west where the darkness comes, toward the north where comes the frost, and last down to Mother Earth from which all things grow. He prayed, "Our Great Spirit, who is the Great Mystery, the Maker of the sun, moon, stars, earth, water, including the human upon the land of the earth, bless me, to gain vision and power and the inspiration of the spirit to serve my people."

All of Beaver Valley pleased Crazy Horse, but his most beloved spot was Beaver Mountain. In the vast expanse of the clear, blue sky above, he seemed very close to the spiritual power from which he sought guidance and wisdom. From its top he watched soaring eagles, the highest flying birds, sent by the Great Spirit to watch over him and his people. To be always ready and available, the eagles nested in the nearby pine trees.

Howard Red Bear said that at the time of Crazy Horse, the Rosebud Band and some of the Oglalas camped in Beaver Valley. Nobody really claimed the area, but the Rosebuds always chose the upper part and the Oglalas, among whom were Red Bear's parents, camped downstream.

Fast Thunder's people always camped where the south branch joined the main valley near the beaver dam. It was a good place, somewhat elevated, giving them a view of the camps of their friends. Mrs. Fast Thunder, also known as Wounded Horse, told her daughter, Mary Pacer, that the tipis would have been set in a circle in open country, but in the hills and narrow valleys this was impossible, so the people chose convenient spots. She had especially liked this one because it was a place where their people could easily come together to visit or to sing. And when the men weren't out hunting, they often gathered to discuss tribal affairs and make plans for the future.

The location of Fast Thunder's camp can still be recognized. The mounds of dirt on the upper side next to the hill must have been left after the floor of the tipi was leveled and the inside fireplace dug out. A travois trail from the west came along by the north side of the tipi and continued around the beaver dam. From the dam, the trail, still plainly visible, goes along the hillside through the pine trees for about a mile up to the old ceremonial grounds.

The little red pipe that meant so much to American Horse was found by Everette White Dress across the travois trail from Fast Thunder's camp on the west bank of the creek in 1957. About three inches long and slightly more than an inch across, the pipestone pipe is modeled after early, straight bone pipes and is inscribed with two sets of inverted *v*'s and five raised circles. Its stem was a faint line on the ground, possibly rotted bone.

To the Indian, a man's pipe was a special possession, honored at all times as was everything associated with it—stem, pouch, tobacco. Some pipes were plain, but most were carved with designs or

Fast Thunder, photographed by Charles M. Bell. (*Smithsonian Institution National Anthropological Archives*)

decorations representing significant facts. Although different pipes were used for different reasons, the straight pipe was used solely for ceremonial or religious purposes. It formed the communication link with the Great Spirit. Sometimes, in order to commemorate a special ceremony, the men smoked, then refilled the pipe and left it as a marker with a surrounding tobacco line—a string of rawhide to which were attached, one after another, pinches of tobacco in individual bits of buckskin.

We have wondered if it was after such a ceremony long ago that the little pipe was left on the hillside. Do the inverted *v*'s carved on its sides represent Beaver Mountain and its twin? Do the five raised circles have any connection with the five strange rocks that lie on the ceremonial grounds at the foot of Beaver Mountain? Could this have been Crazy Horse's pipe, left by his mother after she had spent the night after the burial smoking and singing the death chant?

A second well-known camp was that of Brown Cap (or Brown Hat), who got his name from the brown beaver-skin cap he wore. According to his granddaughter, Julia Hollow Horn Bear, he was an Indian historian who kept an important record called a winter count. She said that he had learned to do picture writing from the "beavers" of Beaver Creek. They were the missionaries who had come to live in the valley and who seemed, at least to the Indians, much like the beavers. Their homes were made of logs and plastered with mud like the beaver's lodge. The white men had a doorway and a door; the beaver, a tunnel and water closing it. Inside the man's cabin was a table to hold his food; inside his lodge, the beaver had a special place where he stored and ate his food.

When Brown Cap was invited into their home, the missionaries said, "The whites will be with the Indians, try to get along, Baptiste Good." And thus they gave him a white-man name. He was told that his people would soon live with the white people and speak their language and that they should associate and cooperate, as well as be real friends. "By the cross, the Indians will be converted, for this is the symbol of God," they said, and they gave him a cross made of willow branches.

They also gave him a small notebook and a pencil and taught him to write. They showed him how to make records with a simple kind of writing, which was actually picture writing or drawing. He soon began collecting and recording traditional history that had always been preserved and transmitted orally. Years or longer periods of time were named after significant events. As additions were usually made to the histories in the winter when people had more leisure, the records were called winter counts. Although there are many winter counts, Baptiste Good's record is said to be the only Lakota history depicting events that occurred before 1775.[1] Beginning in 1700, each year had a distinguishing name and an explanation, but before that date he recorded periods of time in cycles of about seventy years, except for the first period of 901 to 930 A.D.

Battiste Good, or Brown Hat, and family. Photo by J. A. Anderson.

The most important event of this first period was the coming or appearance of the White Buffalo Cow, also called the White Buffalo Woman, although the "Dakota were a people long before this."[2] According to the legend, a beautiful woman approached the Dakota Nation when all of its people were living together. She came to teach the people how to live and gave them a pipe and a small package containing four kernels of maize—one white, one black, one yellow, and one variegated. She indicated she would scatter these over the earth "that the people may live by it." Always afterward, they kept the pipe as a remembrance and as a means of communicating with the Great Spirit.

Garrick Mallery recorded this information in 1893. He said that Baptiste, or Battiste Good, as he was more commonly called, was given a paper notebook by Reverend Wm. J. Cleveland who was in charge of the Episcopal Mission and school established at the Spotted Tail Agency when it was located on west Beaver Creek. In the notebook Battiste Good made a facsimile of his original record. He used black and other colors, but none had any significance except the red for blood. Mr. Mallery indicated that the records were acquired (how, he doesn't say) and that Good added a few embellishments of his own including English words and Arabic numerals in a kind of meddlesome vanity. Yet the records have been verified by comparison with other sources, and Mallery concedes that "notwithstanding Battiste's mythic cycles and English writing, the body of the record, which constitutes the true Winter Count, must be regarded as genuine." Battiste Good was simply a bad editor of a good work. Although his work may have been criticized, it is invaluable. His proud granddaughter often said, "The notebook is the evidence we still have which was given to us by the 'Beavers' of Beaver Creek." (The notebook is still in existence and, though fragile, can still be read. At present it is in the Sioux Indian Museum in Rapid City, South Dakota.)

Frank Kicking Bear knew of a third important camp in the valley, that of Crazy Horse and his parents. Their camp was almost across the south canyon from Fast Thunder's. They liked to live on the

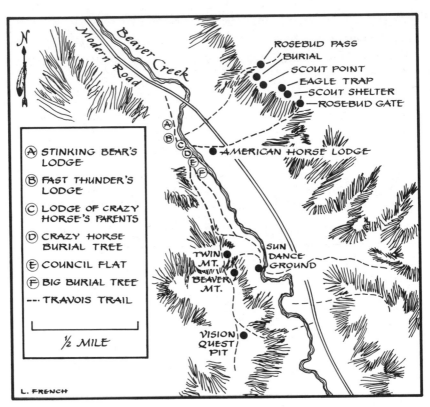

Beaver Valley, Nebraska

V-shaped flat bounded on two sides by water where the beaver dam
backed it up into the south canyon and Beaver Creek. Kicking Bear
said the top of their lodge was blue to represent the sky and the
bottom green to represent the earth. Crazy Horse made a corral out
of pine poles between the travois trail and his parents' lodge where
he kept his pony nearby and safe from thieving enemies.

This wilderness home of Crazy Horse and his band was a village of
about eight hundred conical lodges that stretched about a mile and a
half along both sides of the creek. Although there were many people
here, the most important individuals, according to those who provided this information, were Fast Thunder, the medicine man;

Battiste Good, the historian; and Crazy Horse, the leader. Of these, Crazy Horse was by far the most eminent.

In addition to markers so far mentioned, within the confines of this wilderness camp are others that will be described as this story proceeds. Among these are the Sun Dance grounds, the Burial Trees, and the Burial Site.

3

SPOTTED TAIL AGENCY AND CAMP SHERIDAN

About the time that Crazy Horse assumed leadership of his band, great numbers of white people were passing through Lakota country on their way to the west coast. Many stopped to hunt for gold and to establish permanent settlements. The Indians' efforts to stop this flood of strangers led to years of warfare. As part of the complex arrangements to end the fighting, the U.S. government established reservations, according to the terms of treaties signed with the Indians. Agencies, under the control of church officials, had the job of administering the affairs of the Indians, particularly of distributing rations to the people who could no longer make a living off the land while restricted to the reservations.

The Whetstone Agency, first set up for Spotted Tail's bands on the Missouri River, was moved several times, finally to a place near the mouth of Beaver Creek on the White River. The Red Cloud Agency for the Oglala bands was moved from the Platte River to the White Cliffs country on the upper White River not far from the Whetstone Agency. During the winter of 1873-74, these two small agencies supplied a huge concentration of Lakota people scattered throughout the pine-covered hills south of the White River. They were all in what is now Nebraska, outside the reservation in South Dakota.

Even Crazy Horse's followers, called Northerns by officials because they preferred to lead a free life hunting in the north country, came into the agencies. They demanded rations but continued their customary raiding and horse-stealing from whites and other Indians. During the spring, in order to protect the agencies and control the

marauders, the government established Camp Robinson near Red
Cloud Agency and another army post at Whetstone Agency.

By summer Whetstone Agency had been moved twelve miles up
Beaver Creek and renamed Spotted Tail Agency. Within a year the
agency consisted of "3 dwelling houses, 1 store house, 1 stable, 1
stockade surrounding same, also 1 slaughterhouse and beef corral
connected therewith, and 1 schoolhouse, forming altogether with
the new chapel built by the Episcopalians, a pleasing and convenient arrangement of edifices."[1] The school and church were probably the first established in Beaver Valley. The army post was
also relocated to Beaver Valley, farther south than the agency, "up
in the pines near the Big Spring."[2]

On September 10, 1874, the name of the post was officially
announced as Camp Sheridan. It lay within a mile of Spotted Tail
Agency in a position that overlooked and commanded it. The grassy,
tree-covered slopes of Beaver Valley must have provided a dramatic
and welcome change for the soldiers. Back at White River, the hills
were already dry and brown with bare spots of yellow dirt showing

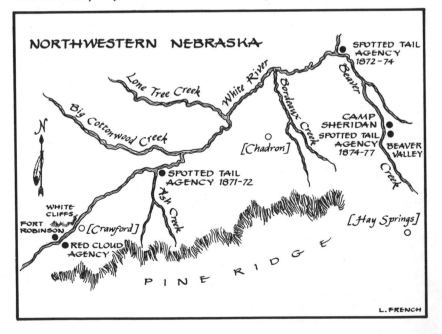

through the sparse grass. There the soldiers had waited through a hot, sticky summer with only flapping canvas tents to cut the summer's heat. In Beaver Valley they found plenty of tall, straight pine trees with which to construct mud-chinked log houses, fifteen feet square, nine feet to the eaves, with roofs of brush and dirt.

The next spring, Captain Anson Mills arrived to take command of Camp Sheridan. Shortly before he came, General Crook had inspected the temporary log huts and had left orders for Mills to select a new location for a five-company post. During the summer of 1875, Camp Sheridan was moved a mile and a half north and downstream. When the work was finished, Captain Mills wrote with satisfaction that "each captain constructed his own barracks and quarters, after plans I prepared, dividing the skilled artisans between them. We were completely housed before the first of October. All the buildings were constructed as a shell of straight inchboards around a framework, lined with ordinary sized bricks, dried in the sun and plastered inside. . . . There were no contracts, no delays in construction and it was probably the cheapest, most satisfactory and most rapidly constructed post ever built by the army."[3]

When some of the Northerns (without Crazy Horse's band) came in October 1875 to spend the winter at the agencies, they already knew that the Spotted Tail Agency under the close protection of Camp Sheridan was not far from their old camping place near Scout Point. Indeed, the area actually lay in the southern part of the Camp Sheridan Wood Reserve. But the Northerns were not afraid of the soldiers because both friendly and hostile Indians completely surrounded the post.

Although the Spotted Tail agent was reassured by the fine new army camp, the presence of the soldiers did not solve all of his problems. Moving the agency Indians to the new location had been a difficult task, and it had hardly been completed before the Bureau of Indian Affairs ordered him to count the incoming hostile Northerns.[4] This was impossible, for he had never been able to count even the friendlies, so he managed to convince the bureau that the project should be put off.

The corral at Spotted Tail Agency, 1877. (*USMA Library, West Point*)

The next directive from Washington proposed to start reducing the power of the Indian chiefs by taking away their right to distribute rations and supplies to their own bands. Agent E. A. Howard doubted if there were enough soldiers at Camp Sheridan to counter serious opposition to such a change.[5] A later census showed that he had been wise, for 9,610 Indians were listed at his agency. To add to the turmoil, forty-five white men who had previously caused trouble had taken up residence near the Spotted Trail Agency,[6] and they could not be ousted. (This problem apparently continued as long as the agency remained in Beaver Valley.)

Then the greatest problem of all presented itself, and no letter of protest from the agent could prevent it. The agency was desperately short of food and the people were hungry. Bitter cold and deep snow had buried the countryside and freighters would not even try to cross the wind-swept plain, billowing in drifting snow, on the long 162 miles from Sidney to the Spotted Tail Agency.

Crazy Horse and Sitting Bull and their bands of Northerns remained aloof from the troubles at the agency and spent the winter of 1875-76 somewhere beyond the Black Hills.

As winter moved toward spring the agents realized that people were leaving, heading north in large numbers. As the army could not stop this movement, they requested that the control of the agencies be transferred from the churches to the army. The agency Indians, or friendlies, were worried about how this proposed change would affect them. Reverend W. J. Cleveland met with them in council and wrote a petition for them to President Grant stating their beliefs. The letter was written at Spotted Tail's lodge on Beaver Creek, on March 8, 1876, and listed several objections to military supervision.

"1st. Soldiers generally are obnoxious to our young men and their dislike for us is so evident as always to provoke ill feeling and mischief on the part of our young men, making it hard for us to control them.

"2nd. We know that a majority of the army is composed of immoral men and the influence of the soldiers, as well as of the Officers, has always been for bad and never for good among our people. They corrupt our women and introduce and encourage among our people the vices of drinking, gambling & C. Thus though we are living at peace with them and they do not fight us with powder and ball, whenever they are located near our people, they bring death to us in other ways.

"3rd. Nearly all the trouble we have had at this Agency since Soldiers were located here has resulted directly or indirectly from them. They have, through their Trader, introduced whiskey among the people here, which act has already resulted in one murder and much other domestic trouble. For these, and other reasons, we are not only opposed to having Army officers for our Agents, but we earnestly hope that the day will soon come when they will be removed entirely from our country."[7]

The petition had little effect, and things went from bad to worse. Having survived the winter without the agencies' help, the Northerns were in no mood to cooperate. With their allies, the Northern

Cheyennes, they annihilated Custer's Seventh Cavalry at the Little Big Horn in June. Crazy Horse, of course, played a leading role in this greatest of Plains Indian victories.

With more pressing matters to deal with, the government did not turn the administration of the agencies over to the military until the fall. A reluctant Congress passed an appropriations bill to feed the Indians at the agencies for another year, but enormous concessions were required of them. The Lakotas had to give up the Black Hills, the Powder River, and the Little Big Horn country and agree to move east to the Missouri River. To secure signatures on the agreement the commissioners met with small groups of people and threatened to withhold rations and to forcibly move the people to the Indian territory in the south (Oklahoma).[8] Although the agreement did not require this move to the south, Spotted Tail consented to consider the proposal. So that winter, he and some of his chiefs made the trip. On their return, he explained his feelings and desires in a formal speech:

"My friends the Indians and whites which are in here, I want you to keep silence, because I want to make a speech. The whites here we consider as Indians and I want them to keep silence, too.

"This speech I am going to make, is not on my account, but it is the wish of the people, for me to make this speech. The Great Father asked me to go to the south to see the country. I listened to his word and traveled 45 days to see the country. When left here to go to the south, I left with the idea to find a good country, for my people to live there and raise their children, to go and live there. I have found nothing good for my people, when I found nothing good for them I have been thinking of a good many things. I made treaty 3 times and the Great Father promised many things which I have not received, also I had a great many different Agents which made many promises to me but I did not receive anything. This country belongs to me, but a great many white rascals came to this country to steal the country from me.

"This country belongs to me and the Great Father wanted a part of the country and I gave it to him, when a man has a great deal of country he sells what he don't want and keep the remainder, in which I wish to stay and live with my people and raise my children. When I travelled and found not a good country I have been thinking about these things. My friends here (the officers) are good and wise men and have a good way to do the business straight for the people. I suppose the Great Father has selected good and wise men for the Great Council this winter, who will decide how my poor people is to live.

"While I travelled south I did not see such fine timber or grass and in such country as we have here. If any man is on any land he sells so much and keeps so much for himself. If I do not speak these words and drop all these things, my people would not live at all. My friends the officers are good and wise men and always straight and what I say I mean you to send to the Great Father. That is the way the white man lives. If he has any land and if he don't sell the property for so much, he goes and fences it or makes landmarks and it remains always, when he goes away and while he is gone and somebody is coming to destroy it and if a man steals the property he gets a man to attend to it for him and who has destroyed the property has to pay for it. I gave some to the Great Father and keep so much for myself and I want your officers to send word to the Great Father that I want to

Camp Sheridan, built under the direction of Captain Anson Mills. (*USMA Library, West Point*)

see him this winter. I wish to settle this business with the Great Father myself and what he says I am going to do, I always listen to his words and what I say is for my people.

"I want to tell you what Bad Hand [Colonel R. S. MacKenzie] and Three Stars [General George Crook] told me before they went to the war, that I must arrest all outside Indians coming from the north and to take their ponies and arms from them and turn them over to the soldiers, also they told us that we must help the Great Father and the Great Father would help us and we would travel a good road and live in peace.

"The rascals in the Black Hills are children of the Great Father and the Great Father knows how many there are and I wish that they should pay $5.00 each man to the Indians. This is all I have to say."[9]

Nothing was accomplished except that the plan of moving the Lakotas to Oklahoma was dropped.

Army officials decided that if Crazy Horse were brought in, the changes in the life and ways of the Indians would be complete. A number of delegations of Peace-Talker Lakotas were sent out to contact Crazy Horse and to coax his people to come in. First a group of thirty volunteers went, then Spotted Tail and several hundred well-equipped warriors went out. Later Red Cloud headed another group, and bands of Northerns finally began coming in.

4

THE LAST SUN DANCE

Crazy Horse eventually brought in his people late in the spring of 1877. When other bands had succumbed to the lure of army gifts and treaties, Crazy Horse had led his band away into the prairies and mountains where they could live and worship in the traditions of their forefathers. They stayed in the open country where a man was important because he had the skill and strength to provide for his family. Crazy Horse had always acted vigorously to protect his people and their lands on the plains, in the pine-covered hills, and in the Black Hills. But at last there was nothing more he could do. His people needed food because the killing of the buffalo had destroyed their food source. It was this, not the army, that defeated him and his men. The government had promised them an agency in the north, so he led his band—proud and undefeated—into Fort Robinson. He came in peace to accept payment for his great country.

Crazy Horse's Northerns were given a campsite several miles northeast of the Red Cloud Agency. It was near Cottonwood Creek, a tributary of White River, and lay between Red Cloud and Spotted Tail agencies, but nearer the former.

Army control brought drastic changes to these people. For the first time the Northerns were subject to another's bidding. In times past when they had come to the agency, they had received rations, then used the items they wanted and disposed of the rest. (They had often dumped out piles of moldy flour and used the sacks to hold chokecherries or turnips.) Now they had no choice—they ate the food and wore the clothing provided by the government. In fact, the government had changed or disturbed nearly every part of their lives: it had taken their horses (their wealth) and left them on foot; it had taken their land and sent them to reservations; it had exterminated the buffalo and fed them stringy beef; it had substituted a canvas tent for their comfortable skin tipis. The government had taken almost everything except their appetites. Their life of industry and hunting was exchanged for an existence filled with talk, quarrels, and hunger.

The only part of their lives untouched so far was their religion, and that gave them courage. It provided a way of comprehending the relationship between their inner being and the outer world. This outer world included everything—from fellow humans to all living creatures, from the earth itself to all the elements affecting it. Directing this relationship was a great, incomprehensible force called *Wakan Tanka*, the Great Spirit, the Great Mystery. This force exists in all things: trees, rocks, plants, people, animals, the sun. So it was that a Lakota warrior, needing help, felt he could call upon the nearest object, because it manifested the presence of the Great Spirit.

Lakota religion embodied standards for daily living: bravery, generosity, fortitude, and wisdom. Physical bravery was necessary to ensure survival, so even a child learned its importance. Generosity was probably the easiest to achieve, for a hunter could usually secure plenty of game for his family and enough to share with the less fortunate. Fortitude was the strength of spirit needed in facing danger when mental pressure was worse than physical pain. Wisdom, the greatest of all, was most difficult to attain. Wisdom implied more than just knowledge; it meant a deep understanding of life and how to deal with people, an understanding not given to all.

In practicing their religion, the Lakota observed seven ceremonial rites. Two of these—the Vision Quest and the Sun Dance—were the most beneficial for the warriors. A Vision Quest was an individual activity, and the Sun Dance was a community affair requiring the efforts of many people to be truly successful.

Only a very brave warrior became a candidate for the Sun Dance, for it meant giving his own body in supreme sacrifice. He must endure the greatest physical pain to ensure that his prayers would be answered—prayers that could, if answered, prevent tribal famine or the death of a dear one, or that could bring fortitude in facing immense odds in an impending battle or help in behalf of a friend deemed more valuable than himself. It was a way of offering all he had—his own body. After being fastened to the Sun Dance pole by long leather thongs that passed through the flesh of his chest, the participant danced for three or four days without food, water, or sleep. Prayers to the Great Spirit were often answered, so the Indians considered the Sun Dance the greatest religious gathering among them in those days.

As the Sun Dance season of 1877 approached, activity filled the camps. If the people had been out in the north country, one great dance would have been held, but now, due to the circumstances and limited transportation, several dances were held. The first was below Red Cloud Agency on a little creek in the Crazy Horse camp.[1] Curious whites from Fort Robinson came to watch. Many of the Indians from the agency joined in, and a group came from Spotted Tail's agency more than thirty miles away. A second dance was started south of Red Cloud Agency, but it fell through for want of dancers (only one appeared).[2] To have a successful ceremony it was necessary to have the backing of a large group, and many people wanted to go to the big dance planned for Chadron Creek. According to William Garnett, it was held at the crossing near the Price and Jenks ranch. Groups from both Red Cloud and Spotted Tail agencies came, with the latter predominating. Garnett said that he was quoting others on this location as he did not attend. However, he bought a horse from Two Strike at the Spotted Tail Agency and sent it with American Horse as a gift of donation for the Sun Dance. George Hyde must have been describing this same dance when he wrote, "In June, the Sioux held the greatest Sun Dance ever seen on the reservation at a small stream they called Sun Dance Creek, about midway between the two agencies. Twenty thousand Indians are said to have been present. The surrendered hostiles in all of their glory—real warriors, who had defeated Crook and Custer."[3]

Regardless of how many other dances were held that summer, the observance of the *last* and *genuine* Sun Dance before the Lakota went on the reservation, according to Alfred Ribman, took place at the foot of Beaver Mountain on the old ceremonial grounds above the main camping area. It was held to honor Crazy Horse, one year after the great victory at the Little Big Horn, and to offer prayers for him during the trying times ahead.

The Sun Dance grounds at the foot of Beaver Mountain.

The level area of the ceremonial ground stretched from the bottom of the cliff at the foot of Beaver Mountain eastward to the bend in the creek. Past the creek, higher ground provided room for more spectators. Westward from the top of the cliff high above the valley floor was another slope extending toward the steep side of the mountain. Cleveland Black Crow said his grandparents had compared this shelf-like clearing to a balcony full of people and horses.

(Edna No Fat, a friend of Dora High White Man, also knew of this spot, for while she was riding around on her horse watching the dance, someone shot at her. She wasn't hit, and she kept her seat, even though her horse jumped. She said that the shot was punishment by her jealous boyfriend, because she had broken away from him.)

On the valley floor a tall cottonwood Sun Dance Pole was set in the center of the dancing area. Offerings of bits of flesh, pinches of tobacco, and a pipe were placed in the hole before the pole was raised. The pole symbolically became the stem of the pipe, providing the communication link with the Great Spirit. The pipe is said to be still buried there.

A large shade was then constructed around the Sun Dance Pole, its roof made of animal skins. As each family group came in, they brought a buffalo skin—some covered with wooly brown hair and others tanned a dusty gray. Those who had no buffalo robes brought elk, bear, deer, or even sewn-together rabbit skins. Nearby were the medicine man's tipi where the main dancers prayed and meditated, the sweat bath lodge for the purification rites, and next to that, the huge fireplace. (The fireplace is still visible, although grass has covered the ashes.)

James Chase-In-Morning and Alfred Ribman knew that five warriors sacrificed their blood and flesh for Crazy Horse at the Sun Dance. All five were blood-cousins of the war chief and realized the desperate plight of a leader no longer allowed to lead. Three brothers—Kicking Bear, Black Fox, and Flying Hawk (sons of Chief Black Fox, also known as Great Kicking Bear)—and two other cousins, Eagle Thunder and Walking Eagle, danced for Crazy Horse and the future. Fast Thunder acted as ceremonial chief and spiritual incision overseer.

Joe Black Elk's grandmother, Little Woman, was there. She lived on Beaver Creek at the time and was still single when she attended the dance. She knew the five dancers and remembered that the main part of the dance lasted for four days. Howard Red Bear's father knew about the dance, although he did not attend because his family had gone north with three others to hunt. Thomas White Face, although still very young, was there with his parents and knew of the dance because his parents had told him about it later on.

Thomas American Horse said he was there and remembered coming with his parents in a spring wagon. He carried a precious memory from his childhood that established an unforgettable marker. He and two friends had wanted to attract the attention of a little girl, so they danced and danced with fast, tricky steps and intricate turns (in the general dance, not the ceremony), but she ignored them completely. Later, she talked to Thomas, but she never did like his friends. Thomas was eleven and the little girl only six. When he was older, Thomas understood the true importance of the dance, for he heard over and over the stories told of Crazy Horse.

Crazy Horse attended the Sun Dance as the honored guest but did not take part in the dancing. He mingled with the people, talking with relatives and friends, many of whom he had not seen for a long time. There was assembled for the duration of the Sun Dance Ceremony the largest gathering of people ever to be at one place on Beaver Creek.

The Sun Dance came to a close, but it was incomplete. The customary raid could not be carried out because the people were under the control of the army. But there was one other satisfying way of finishing the Sun Dance, according to Lakota custom, and that was to set up a commemorative marker for a special occasion. Their ancestors to the east (now South Dakota) had left many small earthworks and light stone works on prominent hills or along streams chiefly as memorials of important tribal events.[4] On this occasion, five large rocks were rolled down from the top of Beaver Mountain and placed around the fireplace in a wide V formation with the opening toward the rising sun. Reverently the rocks were dedicated to War Chief Crazy Horse. They were also a permanent memorial to the devotion of the five tribes of the Lakotas who were represented at the ceremony and to the five warrior cousins who sacrificed their blood and flesh in his behalf. All of the people who took part in the great Sun Dance and the dedication ceremony are now gone, but the marker still stands as evidence of the Sun Dance of 1877.

The following day Crazy Horse prepared himself for his own ceremony—the Vision Quest. It was a solemn occasion when his friends prepared the last fire in the ceremonial fireplace now enclosed by the five rocks. This fire would heat the living rocks so that Crazy Horse could purify himself in the sweat bath. Next he scented and purified his clothes and his pony with the thick smoke from the fragrant sage. Riding his pony to the top of Beaver Mountain, he spent the next four days and four nights fasting and praying. After another purification ceremony under Fast Thunder's direction he completed his Vision Quest.

Although Crazy Horse liked to fast on the top of Beaver Mountain, not all warriors went there to fast. Frank Kicking Bear's father, who was a reliable warrior in Crazy Horse's band, knew of Vision Quest ceremonies that were held in prepared pits by the travois trail on the high ridge, south of Beaver Mountain. One such pit, roughly eight feet square, was cut into a slope not far from the top of the hill. Dirt removed was piled to the side and is now a grass-covered mound. The pit is nearly filled by dirt eroding from its sides and several large pine trees are growing in it.

Beaver Mountain was the site of a fasting ceremony as late as 1942. That year Amos Black Crow brought his family and some relatives from Wounded Knee. For four days and four nights, Amos fasted on the mountain top and prayed to the Great Spirit for the soldiers in World War II.

5

INTRIGUE

While the Indians were busy with their religious activities, government officials laid plans for moving them out of the area. This would be a formidable task, as many people were living in a relatively small area. At Red Cloud Agency there were an estimated nine thousand Oglalas, two thousand Northern Cheyennes, and fifteen hundred Northern Arapahoes. In Beaver Valley at Spotted Tail's agency there were eight thousand Brulés, nearly twelve hundred Miniconjous, and some Oglalas.[1] Providing food and supplies was an enormous job for the two agents and their small staff. The small contingent of troops stationed at the two camps had an even harder time keeping so many people under surveillance and control in that hilly, pine-covered land full of hidden valleys and unknown trails. The military leaders knew that everything would be much easier if all these people were living out on the plains on the Missouri River. Supplies could be handled more efficiently there, and soldiers could be stationed in strategic places or moved quickly to troubled spots.

The previous year, Captain Means of Camp Sheridan thought that he had the solution to the problem: "To bring peace, all ponies, arms, and ammunition must be taken from the Indians."[2] Conceivably, this plan could have worked, but there was a serious flaw—the people at both agencies were hungry! On July 1, 1877, James Irwin of the Red Cloud Agency reported that he did not have enough flour to make the week's issue, even at half rations. Shipments from suppliers were more than a month behind. "The Indians are complaining bitterly, and these supplies should be furnished in larger quantities in order to justify a full issue so that the Indians may rest contented and peaceable."³ Irwin also complained that no preparations for winter were being made either at the two agencies or at the proposed new locations on the Missouri. The prospect of thousands of hungry people with winter coming on demanded immediate action.

Irwin had come to his agency assignment determined to show no sympathy for the Indian people. But when the council leaders had pointed out the injustice of the forced move to the Missouri, he found himself agreeing with them. He reported to his superiors that as the Oglalas and Brulés had come to the agencies and were living in peace, the military should yield a little to the desires of the people they dominated. Of course, Irwin realized that some kind of move must be made, as the land survey had disclosed that both agencies were located in Nebraska instead of north of the line as the 1868 treaty required. The people objected to the evils of river traffic—thieves, gamblers, and whiskey—so Irwin suggested that the government locate their agencies on Little White River, which he had been told had wide fertile valleys with plenty of grass as well as plenty of oak and pine timber.⁴

George Manypenny, a former commissioner of Indian affairs, knowing Spotted Tail's feelings about living on the Missouri, said it was most unfortunate that the men choosing the location had failed to consider the desires of the Indians who knew the country so well. A proper Indian policy would have been based on the assumption that Indians are people and should be treated as such.⁵

In August, approximately seventy warriors, including Red Cloud, Crazy Horse, Little Big Man, Young-Man-Afraid-of-His-Horses and Many Stars, met in a council at Red Cloud to hear a message from General Crook concerning a trip to Washington. Eighteen Indians were to go and air their grievances about the move to the Missouri. Crook said that they should select their best and strongest men for the mission.⁶ The general also promised that all who wanted to could go on a buffalo hunt for forty nights, providing they conducted themselves peacefully and returned at a certain time. At the close of the meeting Mr. Irwin offered three cattle along with sugar and coffee to make a feast, a customary ending for a council.

Young-Man-Afraid-of-His-Horses suggested having the feast at the camp of Crazy Horse. The idea seemed agreeable, but Red Cloud and his followers immediately left the meeting. After talking to Red Cloud's men, Irwin explained to headquarters that as Crazy Horse "had but lately joined the agency it was but right and a matter of courtesy for him to come to them, and they were not disposed to go to him, as such action indicated a disposition to emulate him. He had always been regarded by them as an unreconstructed Indian, he had constantly evinced feelings of unfriendliness towards the others, he was sullen, morose and discontented at all times, he seemed to be chafing under restraint, and in their opinions was only waiting for a favorable opportunity to leave the agency and never return. The time had now come. Once away on a hunt, he with his band of at least 240 braves, well armed and equipped, would go on the warpath and cause the government infinite trouble and disaster. The other Indians these men represented had no confidence in him. He was tricky and unfaithful to others and very selfish as to the personal interests of his own tribe. The ammunition that would be furnished to them would be used for the destruction of the whites against whom they seemed to entertain the utmost animosity."[7]

And thus a plot had been started to discredit Crazy Horse. Red Cloud had reason to be jealous. Several times during the summer, he had been pushed aside while the prestige of Crazy Horse had been bolstered. In particular, Crazy Horse, the hostile, had been enlisted as a scout and made a sergeant, just as Red Cloud, the faithful friendly, had, and on equal footing, too. Yet Red Cloud had been promised he would be recognized as highest officer among the chiefs.[8] So this proposed feast was more than his feelings could stand.

Spotted Tail, too, was jealous of Crazy Horse and didn't want him to go to Washington. "As Crazy Horse was a great warrior and had become world-famous because he was the most notable Indian Leader in the Custer Battle, he was sure in Spot's acute understanding to be the lion of the delegation and to shadow and efface Spotted Tail in the public mind and diminish his influence as a chief."[9]

Little Big Man had also become envious. He wanted Crazy Horse out of the way, and he even had hope of supplanting Spotted Tail. At that time, Little Big Man had more Indians with him than Spotted Tail had.[10]

With all this ill-will building up against him, Crazy Horse, trying in his own way to avoid difficulties, went to Beaver Creek to confer with Fast Thunder. Benjamin Shapp, special agent, apparently knew that Crazy Horse had gone from his camp, for in his report he suggested that James Irwin "submit a statement at once as to Crazy Horse, his whereabouts and any other information he may possess of value concerning him."[11]

Crazy Horse told Fast Thunder of his desire to move over to Beaver Valley. He wanted to be away from the gossip and prying that was going on at Red Cloud Agency. In a talk with his father from Spotted Tail Agency he had wondered "if it might not be better for his people there, with everything done through one man and no rows of moccasin tracks to the agent or the soldier chiefs every day or so, making complaints, working for power. . . . He would try to speak of the Brulé agency to his friend the officer of Fort Robinson . . . . He was looking towards the peace of the Brulé agency."[12] Crazy Horse also wanted Fast Thunder's advice on the proposed trip to Washington. According to Joe Black Elk's information, Crazy Horse had received a verbal message sent by an Indian scout from the army with the promise he was to go.

The two men decided to call a council on Beaver Creek. They would discuss the problems and make sure that the people would be satisfied. Before the meeting, Crazy Horse again went to the top of Beaver Mountain to fast and pray. And at the proposed time he came to the meeting with all of the band—chiefs, camp police, and warriors. As the group of men arrived, they seated themselves on the bluegrass-covered flat south of Crazy Horse's parents' camp near the beaver dam.

Crazy Horse had many followers among these people, for he had always been ready to listen and to help them. Now they listened while he spoke. He explained that he had no desire to go to war, and that he wanted to come here and live in peace. That was why his people had originally come into the agency. He told of messages brought by the scouts, that he was to go to Washington to confer with government officials, and that he was to be appointed as the great chief of all the Lakotas. They considered whether these offers were likely to be true or whether they were just rumors, for it seemed difficult to find where the messages came from.

They also discussed the rumors that harm might come to Crazy Horse. He told his listeners that he held no ill will against any of them, although some whom he believed to be his friends had betrayed him. He had waged war to preserve their rights but had lost, and now they were a conquered people. *"S'ena s'reke,"* he said. "If I ever pass away, the whitemen will take you under their custody as wards." According to Alfred Ribman, he said that at his death his bones would turn to rock and his joints to flint. Then he spoke to his warrior cousins, making a special request. If anything happened to him and he died, his body should be painted with red war paint and then plunged into fresh water, anywhere, and his life would be restored. However, if this was not done, his bones would become stone, but his spirit would still rise.

After Crazy Horse had finished, the men discussed the issues and agreed that Crazy Horse should "declare the end of his war trail." He should go to Fort Robinson to request permission to live on Beaver Creek, then settle down and devote his time to leading his people in the difficult way of peace.

At Red Cloud Agency, James Irwin noticed considerable excitement and talk among the Indians. He asked if he, as a civil agent, could help them, and was told: "We moved our villages together ten or twelve days ago to council upon the various subjects interesting to us. We have held councils everyday and done all we could to quiet 'Crazy Horse' and bring him into a better state of feeling, but we can do nothing with him—he has not attended our council."[13] Irwin was by then completely convinced that Crazy Horse was undependable and so wrote to Mr. Smith that "it now appears that 'Crazy Horse' has not been acting in good faith with the army—He has all the time been silent—sullen—lordly and dictatorial and cruel with his own people and other bands of Sioux at this and at Spotted Tail Agency. He dictates the place for his agency up north and says he is going there—refused to sign receipts for his goods and made other demonstrations about the agency which I reported to the commander of the post and it was hardly credited as the military still had faith in Crazy Horse."[14]

Later on, when General Crook came to Camp Robinson, he called for a council with the chiefs, and again all came except Crazy Horse. Crook explained that it was their duty to control Crazy Horse. The chief deliberated and said that Crazy Horse was such a desperate man it would be necessary to kill him. General Crook replied that that would be murder and could not be sanctioned; but he would count on the loyal Indians to arrest the war chief themselves, as it would prove to the nation that they were not in sympathy with the nonprogressive element of their people.[15]

The military leaders believed that if Crazy Horse were taken away, his followers would be controlled and the move to the Missouri could be effectively carried out. In addition to telling the chiefs to capture Crazy Horse, the officers ordered the scouts to bring him in. The scouts and a large number of other armed Indians and a large force of white soldiers set out to take Crazy Horse. They found his camp abandoned. The people had fled toward Spotted Tail Agency, Crazy Horse among them.[16]

6

TO KILL AN EAGLE

As a rider came around the bend in Beaver Valley, Wounded Horse, Fast Thunder's wife, recognized War Chief Crazy Horse. Fast Thunder immediately asked his wife to prepare a midday meal so he could eat with his cousin. (They always called each other cousin as a term of friendship.) While she cooked, she heard them busily talking but was not able to understand what they said.

Crazy Horse explained to Fast Thunder that he had come to seek good counsel and spiritual guidance. He told of stories being spread concerning his pending apprehension, which could come at any time. He spoke of friends bringing the news that he would be sent to prison and his people moved to the Missouri and now they had begged him to do something to prevent it. He added that besides talking to Fast Thunder, he had come to meditate, because Beaver Valley, having been such an important place to his people, might again bring him peace, or at least peace of mind. Fast Thunder, as an army scout, had already been informed by fort officials that Crazy Horse should come in and he finally suggested that Crazy Horse should appear at Camp Robinson to confer with the commander. Fast Thunder would go along.

There at Fast Thunder's camp next to Beaver Creek, Crazy Horse ate his last meal and drank his last coffee. Then they left camp, Fast Thunder driving his team hitched to a light spring wagon and Crazy Horse riding on the seat beside him, having tied his horse to the side of the team. Fast Thunder's wife rode behind in the back of the wagon. Other friends along the way joined them. Even his parents followed, although they were some distance behind.

At Camp Sheridan they were met by army officials. Later Major Burke and Lieutenant Jesse M. Lee of Camp Sheridan, while riding along, discussed the qualities of Crazy Horse. They agreed that he would become great among his people, because he had never been trained, like the old chiefs, to use diplomacy and persuasion to gain advantages. When he spoke, it was straightforward and honest, and he could be depended on to keep his promises.[1]

As the group approached Camp Robinson, it had grown into a large procession, having been joined by Indian scouts and police and other warriors all along the way. When it passed Red Cloud Agency, the excited agent hurriedly sent off a message to headquarters: "Red Cloud Agency, Sept. 5, 1877. Crazy Horse has been taken. A large body of Indian Soldiers have just passed this agency on the way to the post having him in custody. All quiet."[2]

Orders from Washington had been received at Camp Robinson directing that Crazy Horse be taken into custody. Although some Indians knew it, no one had told Crazy Horse that he was actually under arrest; this news might have caused trouble. About three hundred of his relatives and friends were with him by then.[3]

According to the army's plans, Crazy Horse was to be removed from the camp at midnight and taken by rail to the Dry Tortugas, a group of islands off the coast of Florida.[4]

Quite unaware of the intrigue, Crazy Horse arrived at Camp Robinson and headed toward the commander's office. From the manner in which he walked, it was apparent that he did not know he was to be imprisoned. Though he walked with Fast Thunder, he was actually a few steps behind, and Fast Thunder's wife followed them as she watched the guard on duty walking back and forth. Fast Thunder turned toward the offices. He thought that Crazy Horse was following. But Crazy Horse was escorted by others in a different direction, and he, in turn, believed Fast Thunder was behind him. When he looked back over his shoulder and saw that Fast Thunder was going the other way, he called out in Lakota, "Hey Cousin, you have taken me to the wrong place."

While he was being pushed forward, another Indian, Little Big

Man, caught up and told him that he was being arrested and should defend himself. He would be locked up if he went inside. Crazy Horse thought he was on his way to a conference and couldn't believe the words, yet when he saw the bars on the windows, he knew he was at the guardhouse. When another Indian shouted, "Do something," he drew a knife and attempted to break loose, but Little Big Man held his arms. Watching was a "multitude of Indians trembling with anger, two sides, each with cocked revolvers in hand bending and swaying like crouched tigers ready to spring at each other's throats"—the followers of Crazy Horse on one side and the scouts on the other. All the space in the immediate area around the commissary building and on to Soldier's Creek were "teams, horses, and Indians in a seething mass."[5]

Crazy Horse and Little Big Man struggled. Scouts cocked their pistols, but the officer of the day forbade them to fire. As Crazy Horse gained a bit of advantage and twisted away, Little Big Man received a cut on the wrist. An Indian said to be the uncle of Crazy Horse, moved by his nephew's appeal of "Let me go!" thrust Little Big Man in the stomach with the butt of a gun, saying, "You are always in the way." The blow sent Little Big Man backward to the ground.[6]

Swift Bear, Black Crow, and Fast Thunder grabbed for Crazy Horse to stop the wild struggle. But a white soldier, William Gentiles,[7] lunged at Crazy Horse with fixed bayonet, and the blade pierced him in the side, puncturing his kidneys and passing nearly through his body. Chief Chips, an Oglala, and Chief Turning Bear, a Brulé, grasped his arms to steady him, but the chief dropped face down on the ground, writhing and groaning, while blood gushed from the deep wound. Fast Thunder's wife heard him say, "Cousin, you killed me. You are with the white people!" As soon as she saw Crazy Horse fall, she started singing a death song for him. She took her blanket and covered him up.

Fast Thunder was appalled! He had been instructed (in fact, ordered) to bring in Crazy Horse. And he had done what he had promised to do, but with the understanding that Crazy Horse was coming to a conference, not to a prison or death. He didn't know what to do. He had been lied to. He grew angry with his commanders. If there had not been so many Peace Maker Indians present, he would have given way to his feelings and started a war right there. Confusion reigned. Even the friendlies who had been against Crazy Horse hadn't expected him to be attacked.[8]

Crazy Horse died later that night, and Chief American Horse took charge of the body, wrapping it in a blanket. Later four soldiers brought a spring wagon hitched to a team of mules. Thunder Hawk, with the help of some others, placed the body on the wagon, but it was impossible to find anyone to drive it until at last two Indian scouts volunteered. They believed an outbreak in the camp might erupt and angry warriors would kill those who carried the body. On the way, an Indian said to be the same uncle who had been so handy in laying out Little Big Man leveled his gun at the driver. The frightened fellow promptly fell over into the lap of his companion, who dissuaded the Indian from shooting.[9] The wagon was driven a short distance over the hill east of the camp, and there the man waited for Crazy Horse's father to come and take the body.

Rumors spread quickly. Before Crazy Horse had breathed his last, a story that he had stabbed himself reached Camp Sheridan.[10] Immediately official reports contradicted each other. The next day agent Irwin reported to the Commissioner of Indian Affairs: "Crazy Horse resisted last evening when about to be imprisoned; had concealed weapons; fought furiously and was killed. . . . Little Big Man was wounded by Crazy Horse."[11]

Lieutenant Clark, in his much longer report, gives this account of the killing: ". . . though surrounded by White and Indian Soldiers [he] made a violent effort to cut his way out stabbing Little Big Man (who had hold of him) in the arm and in the scuffle that ensued himself getting stabbed in the abdomen.

"He seemed to think it was done by one of the Soldiers bayonets, but it is impossible to ascertain about the matter as the Doctors from the appearance of the wound thought it must have been done with his own knife. He died at 11:40 P.M."[12]

Eyewitnesses generally agree that Crazy Horse was killed by a soldier's bayonet but differ in the details. Dr. V. T. McGillicuddy said, "I saw him enter the guardroom next door, a prisoner, out of which he sprang without delay, with a drawn knife, to regain his freedom, and I was standing forty feet from him when one of the guards, a private of the Ninth Infantry, lunged his bayonet into the chief's abdomen, and he fell to the ground."

According to Lt. Jesse M. Lee, ". . . just then an infantry soldier of the guard made a successful lunge, and Crazy Horse fell, mortally wounded, with a deep bayonet thrust in his right side!"

Captain Lee's wife, Lucy, said that after Crazy Horse entered the guard house "he threw up his hands and gave a spring toward the door, and at the same time jerked from some hidden place about his body a knife, which he endeavored to use upon the officer, and he would have succeeded had not an Indian, Little Big Man, caught hold of the maddened chief and prevented him from so doing, thereby receiving a flesh wound in his own arm. Crazy Horse still continued fighting his way out the door, and while so doing was bayonetted by a soldier of the guard. He fell to the ground moaning piteously."[13]

William Garnett absolved the soldier from deliberately killing Crazy Horse. "About this juncture the sentinel who had been gazing at the contest brought down his piece and extended his arms at full length as if making a thrust. At the precise instant that this was done Crazy Horse swung himself around towards the soldier with great force in a desperate effort to break loose and the bayonet pierced him in the side, passing nearly through his body and into both kidneys."[14]

He Dog, who had fought with Crazy Horse, was with him when he was killed. "Soon after Crazy Horse had gone into the jail, a noise began in there. Crazy Horse had a revolver with him and tried to draw it, but it was taken away from him. Then he drew his knife. American Horse and Red Cloud shouted to their men, 'Shoot to kill!' The white sentry who was on guard outside the jail ran in behind Crazy Horse as he was fighting with the Indian police and lunged—

twice—with his bayonet. Crazy Horse cried, 'They have stabbed me!' "

Red Feather, the younger brother of Crazy Horse's first wife and a member of his band, was also present. He heard talking inside the guard house; then, "Spotted Tail's scouts cried out, 'It's the jail!' and left Crazy Horse and ran outside. Crazy Horse drew his knife and started to follow them. Little Big Man, who had promised the soldiers to stay with Crazy Horse, caught his hands and held them behind his back. Crazy Horse cut his wrists as they were fighting for the knife. The sentry came in behind them and ran Crazy Horse through once. The thrust went through the kidneys. This was done a little before sunset."[15]

Whatever the details of Crazy Horse's killing, the fact was that the great war chief was dead. It but remained for his parents to take his body into the night.

7

CRAZY HORSE'S LAST STOP ON BEAVER CREEK

Crazy Horse's parents transferred their son's body from the wagon to their travois. On their way back to Beaver Valley, the pain of their grief was compounded by suspicion of treachery. In every person they met, they saw someone who might try to steal the body. These fears were not entirely unfounded, though they came partly from a terrible misunderstanding.

Right before Crazy Horse had come into Camp Robinson, he was greatly feared, although he was living near the agency and was dependent upon the agent for rations and supplies. At the height of the excitement, a $200 reward had been offered for his capture. Ironically, though the man was killed at the camp, no one was able to claim the reward because he had not been captured.[1]

When his parents arrived at Camp Robinson they heard about the Indian scouts sent after their son and about the reward. There was "a price on his head," they were told, but not understanding the idiom, they thought that someone wanted their son's head and would pay money for it. All the way from the camp they were afraid that someone would still try to cut off his head for the money.

And there probably were some white men who thought they could collect the reward. Julia Hollow Horn Bear said that the old people were followed back to camp by men with just that in mind. In addition, Crazy Horse's father hated the jealous chiefs and scouts who he believed had betrayed his son and didn't want any of them to touch the body.

Everyone in camp grieved, but the five warrior cousins were distraught. In the confusion they had forgotten their promise to Crazy Horse to paint his body with red war paint and plunge it into fresh water so that the chief could come back to life. They had failed him. According to what Crazy Horse had said at the council, his spirit would now rise, but his bones would turn to stone and his joints to flint. Joe Black Elk remembered how as a boy he and his friends had searched the hills for the petrified remains of the chief.

Jesse Romero's grandparents told her that when Crazy Horse's parents arrived at Beaver Valley, weeping friends unhitched the horse for them and led it away to feed and water while others grasped the poles of the travois and leaned them against a tree, keeping the load upright. White-Woman-One-Butte, the eldest daughter of Battiste Good and the aunt of Julia Hollow Horn Bear, washed the dried blood and dust from the body. Even though it was too late for the prophecy to come true, they annointed Crazy Horse's body with red paint and marked him with the designs he wore in battle. They then wrapped him in new deer skins with a large buffalo robe secured with rawhide strings as an outside cover.

During these preparations, Crazy Horse's father began making a Spirit Bundle. As a medicine man, he knew the proper procedures to follow in caring for a dead man's spirit. Joe Black Elk's grandmother told him what the old man did. First, he braided a lock of hair at the back of his son's head and tied it at both ends, then carefully severed it close to the scalp. This braid now contained his spirit. After purifying the lock in the smoke of burning sweet grass, he secured it in a buckskin bundle.

Making a Spirit Bundle or Spirit Keeping was one of the seven sacred ceremonies given to the Lakota by White Buffalo Woman. Caring for the bundle required great personal effort and responsibility. According to Black Elk in Joseph E. Brown's *Sacred Pipe*: "You are now keeping the soul of your own son . . . who is not dead, but is with you. From now on you must live in a sacred manner, for your son will be in this tipi until his soul is released." The father must remember that the habits he establishes will stay with him the rest of his life. He must make sure that there are no arguments or fights in the tipi with his son's spirit and that no bad person ever enters it. Harmony must prevail always because whatever happens will affect the soul. "Your hands are 'wakan'; treat them as such! And your eyes are 'wakan'; when you see your relatives and all things, see them in a sacred manner! Your mouth is 'wakan', and every word you say should reflect this holy state in which you are now living. You should raise your head often, looking up into the heavens."[2]

The big sepulcher tree in winter.

Some of the men selected a "burial tree." Often if the person to be honored was special, a tree within the camp would be chosen. Peter Bordeaux explained that the body would be placed in the branches of the tree overnight and the next day. During this time, warriors would hold a wake, sitting around the sepulcher tree.

Slightly up the creek from the lodge of Crazy Horse's parents was a tree (still standing today) that was often used for this purpose. Thomas American Horse remembered that when he was a boy he had seen at least a dozen bodies on platforms in its branches. But this tree was not used for Crazy Horse, perhaps because he was to be honored above all. The tree his friends and relatives chose stands on the west bank of the creek above the little flat where the council was held. A platform was made of poles and crosspieces tied with rawhide strings and pushed into place as the men twisted two of the branches to the south and three to the north. The branches were spread like the fingers of a cupped hand, protecting its burden.

Crazy Horse's body in its buffalo robe cocoon was reverently lifted up to its temporary resting place. Thomas White Face said that the body rested there through the next day, while Indians gathered from around the area to join in the ceremony. The warriors sat

The Crazy Horse sepulcher tree in 1962.

around the tree singing songs of mourning and war songs and telling stories of Crazy Horse's great deeds.

A feast was held at midnight and again the next noon. After dark the parents and relatives again loaded the body on a travois and the two old people moved off slowly into the night. People thought someone should watch over them, but their desire to be left alone was honored, with one small and very important exception.

The parents returned early the next morning with their hair cut short and ragged. They were bleeding from wounds in their arms and legs where they had cut themselves as a sign of their grief. No one asked where they had buried their son, and the father told them not to look. People again respected their request, and many still say that nobody knows where the grave is.

There have been many suggestions about the location of the grave over the years, and a number of them place it in Beaver Valley. Pete Catches thought that Crazy Horse was buried in the valley. Thomas White Face, Ben Black Elk, and John Galligo were more specific, thinking that the grave is near Beaver Mountain. And Austin Good Voice Flute said, "from what I hear this place is about where Mr. Edward F. Kadlecek lives."

But it turns out that one man had a better idea than the others. He was there. Chief Stinking Bear told the story to his young Osage friend, Lawson R. Gregg, in 1929 or 1930. He told how, "unknown to the father and mother of Crazy Horse, he had followed them out of the camp when they took their son's body off on a travois. He had watched them when they buried Crazy Horse. Crazy Horse, still wrapped in the buffalo hide, was placed, standing up, in a crevice or crack in a bluff. Then they pried and dug with sticks and started a big slide of rocks that completely covered him.

"After they came back, the father went into his tipi. The mother went to a hillside and sat down on a rock. Stinking Bear went to his own folks' tipi and sat beside it where he could watch the old woman doing the death chant. He watched her the rest of the night. She sat where she could see the three black pinnacles along the wall. They were black in the moonlight. They were the marker for her son's

Chief Stinking Bear. (*Nebraska State Historical Society*)

grave. All night long she sat there singing the death chant or smoking a pipe. When morning came she laid the pipe there on a rock."

According to Stinking Bear, the three pinnacles that mark the grave of Crazy Horse are on the west end of the ridge across the valley from the site of Fast Thunder's camp. There are Scout Point and the next two to the northwest, the last being the smallest now hidden by young pine trees. Before the pines grew up there, all three points would have been in plain sight from the camp by the creek.

The three points that Stinking Bear told about. The lowest one, on the left, is now almost hidden by trees.

Just past the third point is a small cliff. At the foot of it is a small, pocket-like enclosure strewn with boulders that have fallen from the cliff. It is possible to see an indentation that could be the top part of a filled-in crevice. The place seems compatible with that described by Stinking Bear.

Along with the pines hiding the point now are several cedars. One is large, shading most of the pocket. Uphill from it are four smaller ones in a line, and below, another one in line with the others. Mr. Gregg said that these cedars may be important and contribute to his belief that he has properly identified the burial place. When he lived near Edgemont, South Dakota, as a boy, he was told that old

Indian people always carried the seeds of this particular kind of cedar with them (this cedar looks more like a bush than a tree). They often planted the seeds at a burial, and he remembered seeing several old burial places marked with such cedars.

Mr. Gregg spent some time walking around the area in the fall of 1979. In recalling the details of Stinking Bear's story, he reasoned that the two old people could not have carried their son's body, as they were alone. It would have been necessary to take it to a place that could be reached by horse and travois. The cliff base would have been accessible. They could have followed the travois trail (still visible) up the hill from the camp and through Rosebud Gate and from there to the cliff.

Crazy Horse's father knew that after the body of his son was removed from the tree and placed in its final resting place, it would be absorbed by the earth, the rain, and the four winds. Yet until that time, he wanted it protected. Perhaps, like a mother bird who flops helplessly in front of a predator until she has led it away from her nest, the elder Crazy Horse and his people allowed false stories of the burial place to spread in order to lead potential danger away from the actual grave.

Looking down into the possible burial area. Rocks have fallen, or were pushed, from a small cliff in foreground. (*Alderman Photography, Rushville, Neb.*)

8

THE LAKOTAS LEAVE BEAVER CREEK

When Crazy Horse was killed at Camp Robinson, his people were terrified. Throughout the night of his death they hastily packed their belongings and fled to their friends at Spotted Tail Agency. A week later the agent there reported that around eleven hundred Indians had "stampeded from Red Cloud."[1]

Although the northern Indians were wildly excited over the death of Crazy Horse, the others at the agency became subdued because they feared the future, brooding over the government orders that they get ready to move to the Missouri River to live. Their regular rations and annuities had already been shipped to that location.

Lieutenant Lee sent in a report of strong protest and support for the Indians, declaring that if the move were made it would undo the work of years. Calling Spotted Tail "one of the best Indians that ever lived," he quoted the chief's words and said that "what he has done for peace entitled him to be heard." Spotted Tail said: "What do they send everything there for? I am not going there. . . . If everything is sent there and I am told to go, the Government will have to keep it, for I tell you this, so you may know about it, I have not yet selected a place. I will first see what rations and annuities I am going to get for my people and after I find that out I will select a place, until that time I am going to stay here."[2]

But the government listened to no one's words. Officials inexorably pushed toward their goal. Congress helped, stipulating in the bill appropriating money for that year's supplies that they be shipped only to the Missouri. In September the delegation of Indians returned from Washington somewhat mollified with the promise that in the spring they could return to White River along Big White Clay Creek and Wounded Knee Creek. So in the end there was no resistance.[3]

Some of the people at the two agencies were allowed to remain in the west. The Arapahoes received preferential treatment because of "their steady loyalty to the government through all the troubles with the Sioux and Cheyenne."[4] The Spanish-speaking people on Dry Creek also stayed. Trail drivers from Texas had brought cattle up for the Lakotas, and some had married Indian women and settled down. Later the government paid them to move onto the reservation. (John Galligo said his parents received eight hundred dollars. Descendants of these people still live on the reservation, and family names such as Galligo, Mesteth, Calico, Pablo, Sierra, and Hernandez were well known.)

A removal date was finally set, and about six weeks after the death of Crazy Horse, the people started travelling. Mr. Irwin from Red Cloud reported: "On the 27th of October 1877, the caravan, consisting of about 4600 Indians, two companies of cavalry, 120 transportation wagons, 200 beef-cattle, and the employees and traders took up the line of march. . . . The weather proved mild for this season of the year, notwithstanding much suffering was experienced. The Indians were poorly clad, not having received their annuities. The river filled with quicksand, and running ice had to be forded three or four times a day."[5] While this caravan of Red Cloud's people followed the course of the White River, the one from Spotted Tail went east from Beaver Creek and stayed further south. Their conditions were no better.

When they reached the forks of the White River, Red Cloud's people refused to go on. Already many of the Northerns had left the group and headed north to the area around what is now Interior South Dakota. Others went over to Spotted Tail's group.

Spotted Tail's people had crossed Wounded Knee Creek about six miles south of the later site of the Wounded Knee Massacre. They wintered on Rosebud Creek, a tributary of White River in southern South Dakota. The following spring they continued east to the old Ponca Agency.[6] (The Poncas had been moved to Oklahoma to make room for Spotted Tail's people.)

The Indians confidently expected to be returning west before long, but reluctant government officials delayed action. Late in the summer the Indians made their own plans for the journey, and in September Irwin notified his superiors that the Indians could no longer be held on the Missouri. Whether the government was willing or not, they were on their way.

Spotted Tail's band stopped on Rosebud Creek and settled on what would become the Rosebud Reservation. Red Cloud brought his people further west to Big White Clay Creek and settled on what would become the Pine Ridge Reservation. Their migrations were over.

The story arose that Crazy Horse's parents took their son's body with them on their long trek, but descendants of Crazy Horse's followers—Standing Elk, Running Bear, and Fat Crane—denied that this was so. They did carry the Spirit Bundle with them, however, and this may be the origin of the story.

The parents observed the proper rituals on the trip, and the year's vigil was completed in the fall when they arrived back on the Rosebud with Spotted Tail's people. Shortly after their return, the ceremony of Spirit Keeping was held. Before a gathering of people from the camp, the medicine man asked the blessings of the Great Spirit through the medium of the sacred pipe. Special food, *wasna*, was prepared for the occasion. With careful ritual, the spirit within the bundle was released toward the south where, according to tradition, it entered the realm of *Wakan Tanka*.

Standing Bear witnessed the event as a young boy, but did not understand it. He described the mysterious impression it had on him: "When we arrived at our destination, the parents of Crazy Horse still had the travois covered with the skin; but they did not build up a tripod at this time. One day we heard that the parents had opened this bundle which was supposed to contain the body of their son, and there was nothing but rags inside! What had they done with the body and where was it buried? Nobody could tell. It was a secret of Crazy Horse's family."[7]

Crazy Horse's mother died two years after her son's death, and his father a year later. They were buried on the banks of the Rosebud.[8] Fast Thunder returned to Pine Ridge with Red Cloud and later served in the U.S. Army as a scout. He successfully brought in part of Crazy Horse's band, which had stayed in the north, and in 1888 went to Washington with a delegation to discuss the division of the reservation into allotments. He chose a piece of land three and a half miles north of Wounded Knee and lived there for the rest of his life.

During his active years, Fast Thunder sometimes displayed a violent temper by riding into town and shooting his gun. Mathew King, as a young man, became very close to his grandfather and often heard the old man's angry words about the government's lies and treachery and about how he and others were deceived by both the army and certain Lakotas into taking part in the plot against Crazy Horse. Toward the end of his life, Fast Thunder spent more and more of his days sitting dejectedly along the banks of Wounded Knee Creek, muttering defiantly to himself. Occasionally, he would stamp the stock of his rifle on the ground and shout in an anguished voice, "They fooled me! They fooled me!"

9

EPILOGUE

More than a hundred years have passed since the Oglalas and Brulés with their famous leaders Crazy Horse, Fast Thunder, and Spotted Tail last followed the trails along Beaver Valley, but their descendants still come to visit. In 1969, a group of people from the Rosebud and Pine Ridge reservations came for a special occasion.

On the evening of June 30, Henry and Leonard Crow Dog, medicine men from Rosebud, and their helpers and families held a Yuwipi Ceremony on the ceremonial grounds along Beaver Creek. The following morning, another part of the ceremony was held to dedicate the place as the Crazy Horse Memorial Park and to bless this story we have put together with the help of many Indian men and women. The ceremony included the sweatbath, the raising of the flag, singing of the Lakota national anthem, and the planting of a cedar tree as a living monument. And once more, in the old traditional manner of commemorating a special event, they built a white stone marker in the shape of an eagle. It was placed near the five rocks and below the cedar tree, and the manuscript of this book in a green folder had a place of honor on the rock eagle. The final event took place inside the large council tipi when all persons present joined in smoking the ceremonial pipe.

In the afternoon, many local people from Hay Springs, Rushville, and Gordon, Nebraska, came to take a walking tour up the valley to the Sun Dance Grounds. After an explanation of the ceremony that had taken place, the visitors were entertained with an Indian dance by a group of Indian Cub Scouts from St. Francis, South Dakota, under the direction of Betty Spotted Elk, the den mother, and her father, Leo Spotted Elk. Richard Full Bull sang for the dancing. Then Mr. Full Bull and Chris Eagle Thunder played on the Indian flute and sang Indian songs.

The little red pipe that American Horse held so reverently is symbolic of Beaver Valley. There is no way to know for certain if it is the one that commemorated the last council of Crazy Horse with the Brulé leaders; or if the two inverted *v*'s carved on it represent Beaver Mountain and its twin; or if the five circles stand for the five rocks, the five warriors, and the five bands of Teton Lakota who were there. But this much is certain: the two burial trees still stand (though the Crazy Horse tree is now dead); the living rocks still enclose the Sun Dance fireplace; the partially filled Vision Quest Pit and portions of the travois trails remain; and Scout Point and Beaver Mountain still have meaning to the Indian people who know the valley's history.

Overhead the spotted eagles glide across the brilliant blue sky. Deer and wild turkeys haunt the hills and valleys. Beaver Creek, though now quite small, murmurs contentedly beneath its pleasant shade. Its water is still clear and cool and good to drink. A medicine man, stooping to quench his thirst, once exclaimed, "Ah! Water just as it was made by the Great Spirit!"

10

TO STEAL AN EAGLE'S SHADOW

One hundred years ago, Indian people said that Crazy Horse refused to have his photograph taken because he did not want to lose his shadow. Today, people still maintain that his picture was never taken. Yet photographs have been published, even in the form of postcards, purporting to be of the great war chief.

There is little or no evidence to support the authenticity of these pictures. Confusion may have arisen in some cases when old people pointed out to their children and grandchildren someone who *resembled* Crazy Horse. As the remark was passed on, sometimes to white people, the man mentioned may have become identified with the chief. At this late date, it is often as difficult to discover the source of the attribution as it is to find evidence to support it.

Man identified as Crazy Horse by O'Neil Photo of O'Neil,   Unidentified Oglala man, said to be Crazy Horse. Date and
Nebraska. Crazy Horse was a young man when he was killed.   photographer unknown. (*South Dakota State*
(*Authors' collection*)   *Historical Society*)

Unidentified warrior, said to be Crazy Horse. Date and photographer unknown.
(*South Dakota State Historical Society*)

H. W. Daley, Chief Packmaster at Fort Robinson where this photograph was taken in 1876, said that this is Crazy Horse. Stanley Vestal identified him as Flat Iron, and the photographer D.F. Barry said in 1926 that the man is Race Horse, who resembled Crazy Horse.

(*South Dakota State Historical Society*)

This photograph by Stanley J. Morrow has often been mistaken as an image of Crazy Horse. However, the man is clearly identified on the back of the Morrow stereoscopic card as Crazy In The Lodge, "head warrior under Spotted Tail."

(*W.H. Over Museum*)

PART II

STATEMENTS

The following statements were acquired over a period of several years. Edward Kadlecek and David Long (Black Cat) interviewed American Horse, Blacksmith, Eagle Heart, Good Voice Flute, High White Man, Pacer, Hollow Horn Bear, George Red Bear, White Dress, and Wolf Ears. The interview with American Horse was conducted entirely in Lakota, the others in a mixture of Lakota and English. Long was responsible for transcribing the tapes, translating the Lakota, and supervising the typing.

Joseph Black Elk wrote his own statement, as well as Bordeaux's and Red Star's after talking with them. Pete Catches talked with Ribman in Lakota and wrote out his statement for him.

Joe White Face wrote his own and his father's. He translated Howard Red Bear's statement as he talked and then transcribed it. He also translated a Lakota tape made by Kicking Bear and Fire Thunder.

King's statement was taped in English. Fire Thunder wrote his in Lakota. Chase In Morning, Crow Dog, Iron Shell, Swift Bird, Black Crow, White Buffalo Man, Gregg and Red Cloud were interviewed and statements prepared by the author.

All the people either read or had read to them their statements to make certain that the final form accurately reproduced what they wanted to say. Each person then signed his or her statement before a notary public.

Statement

Interpreter: Tell what you know about Chief Crazy Horse.
American Horse: Yes I know. I will now tell here what I know about Chief Crazy Horse. From north where Crazy Horse was staying he

Thomas American Horse in 1890.

was brought back by another Indian with the understanding that he is to meet some officials in Fort Robinson. As Crazy Horse and his companion Fast Thunder entered the military post Crazy Horse was taken into custody unknowingly by him. And as he was taken to the guardhouse, he noticed the bars on the door. One Indian companion called to his attention and said they are going to put you in prison so you must do something and he was walking with Fast Thunder, but he walked ahead a few steps and Fast Thunder's wife walking behind them. And when Crazy Horse heard what the other Indian said he attempted to break loose from the guards but another guard carried a rifle with a bayonet attached stabbed him in one kidney. And Crazy Horse said leave me alone, you have killed me. So as they let him loose he fell face down on the ground and died soon afterwards. And as he lie there Fast Thunder's wife took her blanket and covered him up. And soon after that American Horse went back to the camp and brought with him an Indian blanket and spread it on the ground and put the body on the blanket and wrapped him up. Of course, when Crazy Horse's father heard the sad news he went to the fort with a travois and demanded that he be permitted to take his son's body, which the request was granted. So he took the body away. Now where Chief Crazy Horse was killed the Indians supposed to own the radius of 100 miles surrounding the place and I can prove what I have said as Crazy Horse has given his life there.

Interpreter: Thomas American Horse, can you sing?

American Horse: Yes I can sing. (sings) "Crazy Horse your people are depending upon you so you must be courageous and defend your people."

Furthermore I wish to tell you that I am here at Edward Kadlecek's place on the Beaver Creek where Crazy Horse's body was honored by his people by an honoring wake. My name is Thomas American Horse 96 years old, and this is a true statement. I am asking help from all those who read my statement for help. As I have stated we supposed to own 100 acres and retain same area for the Oglala Sioux, who are now residing in Pine Ridge reservation who are some of the Crazy Horse people. And we believe that there is a Great Spirit who can help us. I am now 96 years old but I am still trying to help get some of our land back.

THOMAS AMERICAN HORSE
October 12, 1962

Life of Warrior Chief Crazy Horse

The personal appearance of warrior chief Crazy Horse was light complexion, brown eyes, dark hair, weight about one hundred fifty pounds, height five feet, five inches, thirty-three years of age at the time he was killed. He originated in the great north plains. He was a famous warrior beginning in his age of seventeen years, and the Sioux in a ceremony of purification declared him to the deity of the brave. Later he became a hero of battles of war against enemies and the Sioux observed another ceremony and ordained him to a warrior chief. He was a valued warrior supreme, a keen-eyed fighter, and horseman of distinction. He combed his long hair freely and let it wave in the breeze. He tied two eagle feathers on his head. He tied one eagle feather to the tail of his pony. He wore his war necklace containing bullet proof medicine. He held his weapon—a war club—aloft. He blew his eagle bone whistle and started into the battle. He killed every enemy he caught by knocking them on the head. He rode the fastest running pony in the country. He acted with ambition and vigor to protect and defend the people of the Sioux Tribe against the enemies.

The pony of warrior chief Crazy Horse could last two days of running in the battles. On certain times during the battles he rested on the top of the highest hill for his pony to take the breeze and the pony gained fresh power to run again. No enemy bullet ever hit warrior chief Crazy Horse and his pony. He gained twenty-two battles of war during his war trail. It is believed that the inspiration of the spiritual connected his soul, mind, and physical being, when he fasted on the top of the high hill in the great plains for four days and nights where he prayed to the great spirit for vision and power to serve his tribe. He held his peace pipe up toward the ark of the great spirit in the heaven, toward east from where the light comes, toward south from where the warm comes, toward west from where the dark comes, toward north from where the freeze comes, and downward to mother earth where all things grow and seed. He prayed the following language: "Our Great Spirit who art in heaven, the maker of Sun, Moon, Star, Earth, Water, and all things thrown upon the earth and under the water, including the human on the land of the earth. BLESS ME TO GAIN VISION AND POWER to serve and defend the people of my Tribe." And his gifts of vision and power made him a valued warrior supreme and feared of.

He observed the sweat bath ceremony and fumigated his war costumes and his war pony with the ceremonial scent smokes of burning perfume fragrant before he took part in every battle of war.

Warrior chief Crazy Horse was an Indian's Indian. He never made any peace with the whiteman, but protected his tribe.

He moved in to the chosen land at Beaver Creek and lived with his people the Sioux. The north half of the camp at this place was occupied by the Oglala and the south half of the camp was occupied by the Rosebud Sioux. The said place—the chosen land—was covered with heavy timber of all kinds of trees, served as a place of good protection and safety to camp, and provided plenty of food and good water.

Crazy Horse and his Sioux Tribe roamed in the country around the Rocky Mountains, in the country of Montana, North Dakota, South Dakota, Nebraska, Wisconsin, and Minnesota. In the center of this vast country the mystic Black Hills were the thriving hunting grounds of the Sioux, where the deer, elk, antelope, and buffalo nibbled the sweet mountain grass, watering on the streams of water that ran noisily down through the high walled canyons, with colored cliffs sheltering the valleys. The said animals were the Sioux supermarket, on the hoof, furnishing them with food, clothing, shelter, and even medicine.

Crazy Horse and his warrior band vigorously protected and defended the people of the Sioux Tribe against the invading whiteman

Joe Black Elk.

and the soldiers of the United States Army, who invaded their country, destroying their food, their culture, and their very existence.

The Long Hair—General G.A. Custer—commanded his cavalry division of the United States Army into the vast country again to invade the Sioux, their hunting ground and to abuse the children of the prairie.

Warrior chief Crazy Horse and his warriors mounted on their ponies and rode against the Cavalry of the United States Army, and wiped out the entire cavalry in one hour's time, on June 25, 1876. There were no survivors of General G. A. Custer's gallant division; only one Crow Indian scout escaped with a famous cavalry horse that served a captain of the cavalry, by disguising himself as a Sioux, letting down his hair and wrapping himself in a blanket.

JOSEPH BLACK ELK
March 7, 1966

Dedication of Warrior Chief Crazy Horse— "End of His Trail"

Warrior chief Crazy Horse and the Sioux Tribe returned to the White River area and to the chosen land at the Beaver Creek to dwell. The Sioux moved into the said area from various parts of the great plains. The Sioux consisted of hundreds of tipis with a population of about sixteen thousand.

In the Beaver Valley area there is a mass of big hills stretching in a distance of several miles in the direction of north and south on the east side of the Beaver Creek called Beaver Walls. There is a high white butte standing on the south part of the Beaver Walls. A person can see many miles away from the top of the white butte. It projects conspicuously above its surroundings. The Sioux warriors took turns on duty of scout on the top of the said butte. It was called Scout Point.

Beaver Mountain is located south of the Sioux Camp at the Beaver

Creek. The Sioux warriors observed the Sun Dance prayer ceremony at the foot of the Beaver Mountain. Five warriors ceremonially offered their flesh and blood as extreme sacrifice to the Great Spirit on behalf of warrior chief Crazy Horse. The Sun Dance prayer ceremony was observed four days. On the following day Crazy Horse observed the sweat bath and fumigated his war costumes and his war pony with the scent smokes of burning perfume fragrant, and rode his pony up to the top of the Beaver Mountain and observed a fast.

There are five large rocks set within the area of the Sun Dance ceremony at the foot of the Beaver Mountain. These rocks represented the five warriors that sacrificed their flesh and blood. Another large one set within the said area represented the offering where the sacrifice and the ceremonial peace pipe rested over the nights. These large rocks are still there at the arena of the Sun Dance prayer ceremony up to date.

Crazy Horse at one time dwelled in the north part of this camp. One bright morning in September of 1877, he visited his friends at the south end of this camp. He received a verbal message of agreement sent by an Indian scout from the United States Army Post with the promise to be sent to Washington, D.C., to be appointed as a great chief. He was satisfied with the agreement and decided to devote his time as a leader of the Sioux Nation and also agreed to settle down on a reservation with his Sioux Tribe, so went to the said Army with Fast Thunder and other relatives. The deal of the agreement was unknown to his own folks until later. They also noticed that Chief Crazy Horse, with some other Indians, rode in a buggy and team, traveled toward the west. His folks followed him a distance of some miles behind.

Warrior chief Crazy Horse went to Fort Robinson—the Army Post of the United States Military. He went from the Sioux camp at the Beaver Creek to the said Army Post to meet the commander. As he appeared before the Army Post, a Sioux by the name of Little Big Man advised him that he was bound to be locked up in the guardhouse. As he resisted, away from behind of his back, the cold steel

bayonet speared in his ribs and he died, on September 5, 1877, at
the age of thirty-three years. Four soldiers loaded the body on a
wagon attached to a team of mules and hauled the body to a place
over the hill east of the Army Post. When his own folks arrived at the
said Army Post, they found the dead body of Chief Crazy Horse
lying on the ground in the draw over the ridge east of the Army Post,
under cover of his own war blanket, covered by his friends. Fast
Thunder as a leader, with the parents and friends loaded the body on
a travois and traveled back to the Sioux Camp at the Beaver Creek
through the dark of the night. The body rested at the Sioux Camp on
the next day, where the Sioux warriors honored the body. When the
dark of the night came, the parents loaded the body on the travois
and led off into the dark, and no one ever knows where the body was
buried. This was to keep the body in secret to avoid stealing of the
body by the U.S. Army.

There is a gap on the north end of the Beaver Walls called Sunset
Pass through where the Oglala Sioux moved to the place now Pine
Ridge Indian Reservation. On the south end of the Beaver Walls is a
pass called Rosebud Pass where the Rosebud Sioux moved to the
place now Rosebud Indian Reservation, after warrior chief Crazy
Horse was killed.

JOSEPH BLACK ELK
March 7, 1966

History of the Living Rock

The Sioux Indians prayed to the said Rock. When this whole
country was under water, the living Rock was the first to make its
appearance above the water. All animals, animal life, human life,
and vegetation on the land and under the water comes from the
Rock.

This was the special Rock used in their ceremonies. In the days of
their Happy Hunting Grounds, they obtained five pieces of good
size Rock from the high Rocky Mountains where there are no tracks
of even a bird, but extra fresh Rock. They prayed to these Rocks at a

special Sun Dance Ceremony, for four days. They painted these Rocks with Indian Paint, painted one Rock with red Indian Paint. It stands for the Great Spirit and was placed in a wonderful place at the extreme North of this country, painted one Rock with yellow, stands for the Sun, placed it at the extreme East, painted one Rock with white paint and placed it at the extreme South. The white painted Rock stands for all the animals living on this earth. They painted one Rock with black, stands for the night's rest and placed it at the extreme West. They placed a plain Rock at the Center of the country, stands for the humans living on this earth.

The tribal councils, warriors, and all medicine men and women had a ceremony to establish the title and name of these Rocks. They named each one of the Rocks Grand. Each place of the GRAND or Rock is the domicile of the Almighty and his Spirits to be on Earth. Every member of the Tribe individually prayed to the GRAND day and night to gain the spiritual life for the GRAND and the people. The whole Tribe prayed on special ceremony twice a month. Four selected men including one medicine man was sent out to the location of these GRANDS in the four directions, to worship the GRAND four times a year. The Sacred Pipe was used to pray. They filled the Sacred Pipe up with tobacco and lighted up to smoke. First they touched each one of the GRAND with the Sacred Pipe and then started to smoke and pray. When they finished the prayer, they finished the Sacred Pipe, too. All persons of the Tribe conducted themselves in the condition of gentle life in order for the GRAND to gain spirits.

Some medicine men and women still today pray to the GRAND when they are giving Indian medicine. Also as of to date, some Indian people pray to the GRAND in the Indian Sweat Bath Conic Tipi in the Indian Sweat Bath. The Rocks are heated in the fire and when the Rocks are red hot, they were dropped into the five inches deep and 18 inches wide round hole in the center of the conic tipi, in which about seven persons have room. These persons went inside and sat down around the heated Rocks. They smoke the Sacred Pipe and pray to these heated Rocks, sing the medicine man song, and then one person dips water from the packs and sprinkles it on these red hot Rocks and the steam starts for the bath. When they finished the bath, they pray to the Rocks before they go out.

All the life of the animals and human beings found refuge in the Living Rock and now the animals and human beings are living today. For this reason the Sioux Indians pray to the Living Rock.

This Rock is in Beaver Valley. Beaver Mountain contains ledges of the Rock and is capped with it. From Beaver Valley Indians carried it all over to use for starting fires, cooking, and sweat baths.

JOSEPH BLACK ELK
November 19, 1973

Talk of John Black Smith

I am John Black Smith, age 85, Post Office, Oglala, South Dakota. My father is a member of Cheyenne River Sioux and my mother is a member of the Oglala Sioux. At the time when a monument of Chief Crazy Horse was to be erected in the Black Hills, people from Cheyenne River came. They all saw the sketches of Crazy Horse's looks. They disagreed. Anyway, it was carried on.

Now, the only thing that bothers me is this, I was born in the month of March, and that fall, along in September, Chief Crazy Horse was killed. My only wish, is, that I was born earlier. At any rate, my folks say at the time that Chief Crazy Horse was killed, people all moved out of Fort Robinson and they scattered. Some went through Beaver Creek and White River. They traveled through White Clay Creek to Manderson, etc. Chief Crazy Horse's body was moved through Beaver Creek. No one knows exactly where he was buried. Several years ago a rumor started that Chief Crazy Horse was buried near Manderson, South Dakota. About that time my grandchild died. We brought a casket from Pine Ridge Agency. Upon arrival home we found a skeleton in the coffin. We traded it back to the Agency and found it was supposed to be Crazy Horse. Later, we found that this was not true. Mr. Everette White

Dress found a pipe with carvings at Mr. Edward F. Kadlecek's place. Each carve represents a war. This pipe is one of the earlier pipes they used to smoke with.

JOHN BLACK SMITH
April 29, 1964

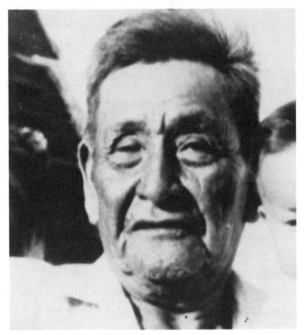

John Black Smith.

Statement

Peter Bordeaux, 89 years of age, a member of the Oglala Sioux Tribe, states that warrior chief Crazy Horse was a valued and superior warrior who protected and defended the Sioux Tribe, their food, their clothing, their shelter, and their wealthy existence.

Crazy Horse stated that if the Black Hills were not covered with great timber it would be shining and bright as the sun from the rays of the gold, silver, and other precious stones of all types. But its yield of timber shaded the Hills black in order to preserve the life of the resources and its related valuations.

Warrior chief Crazy Horse fabricated a medicine of dried heart and brain of an eagle, mixed with dry, wild aster seed compound to make a bullet proof medicine. He wrapped the bullet proof medicine in tanned deer skin and tied it to his war necklace. Before he started in to the battle he put the war necklace on around his neck, dusted the mane and tail of his war pony with mole hill dirt, and blew his eagle bone whistle and took off into the battle. No enemy bullet hit him or his war pony.

The great battle man met sharp and sudden death by the cold steel of a soldier's bayonet speared into his ribs from behind his back by a guard directed by a Sioux Scout.

Chief Chips, a member of the Oglala Sioux Tribe, and Chief Turning Bear, a member of the Brulé Sioux Tribe, held Crazy Horse on each of his arms to help him lay down when he was bayoneted.

Peter Bordeaux.

Lewis (Mato) Bordeaux, a member of the Rosebud Tribe was there, too, at that time. Lewis (Mato) Bordeaux was interpreter between the Sioux and the Army in those days.

The famous warrior Crazy Horse was killed at Fort Robinson Army Camp on September 5, 1877. The parents and relatives of Crazy Horse brought the body back to the Sioux Camp at the Beaver Creek on the same night. The body was elevated upon the branches of the sepulcher tree as a temporary scaffold over the night and the next day.

The warriors observed the wake in the honor of the body over the night and the next day, by sitting around the sepulcher, and when the dark of the next night came, the parents and relatives of Crazy Horse loaded the body up on the travois and led off into the dark of the night and no one ever knows what became of the body.

At that time the Sioux warriors still dressed in tanned deer-skin custom shirts and leggings, with tanned buffalo skin moccasins. The Sioux women dressed in tanned deer-skin dresses. The soldiers of the United States Army dressed in blue uniforms.

Crazy Horse conferred in an assembly with all of the band chiefs, sergeant-at-arms, and the warriors and discussed and decided to declare the "end of his war trail" when the Government of the United States promised him to be appointed as the great chief of all the Indians of the United States. He was killed in a very few days after the assembly had convened.

There were some white eagles, twice as large as the ordinary eagles, that increased and existed in the air and space above the vast country and nestled on the land of the Black Hills all the time prior to the year of 1875. A warrior observed the ceremony of the fast on the top of one of the Black Hills; on his third day, one of the said white eagles flew down and landed on the altar hill by the fasting warrior and talked to him in plain Sioux language. It said that the white men will invade your Black Hills in the very near future and will take over the resources under their possession and give you a bad time. Then the white eagles relinquished their roaming from the vast country of the Black Hills.

Peter Bordeaux solemnly swears that he saw three of the said large eagles sail in the air above his residence at the White River west óf Rosebud, South Dakota, in the year 1962.

PETER BORDEAUX
June 11, 1969

Events at Beaver Mountain

James Chase In Morning is 77 years of age. He is the son of Stanley Chase In Morning who was 17 years of age at the time that Crazy Horse was killed. Stanley Chase In Morning stated that Crazy Horse was a famous brave and an intelligent warrior, who received vision and power by observing the ceremony of the fast. Crazy Horse served and defended his tribe. He owned two horses to ride. One was a bay and the other was a sorrel. He rode the bay horse in most of the twenty-two battles he won. He made shambles of the army troops of the United States. He had no war bonnet, nor other war dress, except that he wore two bald eagle feathers on his head and a necklace with a tanned deerhide covered flint rock attached on his neck. He had a stone war club, a large knife, and an eagle leg bone flute. He blew the whistle of his flute when he started in the battle. He used the war club to knock the enemies on the head, killing every one he caught. He scalped the victim's head with his large knife and brought the scalp back to the Sioux camp, where the tribe observed the ceremonial victory dance. The scalp was hung by the light of the fire in the center of the dance. They danced until daylight, then burned up the scalp.

Crazy Horse observed the ceremony of the sweat bath in honor of the braves, medicine men, and visionary men, and decided to settle down. He chose that land at the Beaver Creek, and the Sioux Tribe moved and camped at the said place. That place yielded protection and safety for the tribe. Many Sun Dances were held there. As soon as the dance was over each year, the people started planning for the next year, setting a date and a place.

In the summer of 1877, the last real Sun Dance ever held took place on that ground at the foot of Beaver Mountain. That dance was held to honor Crazy Horse and to offer prayers for him. It was held one year after his battle with Custer. There were five warriors who sacrificed their blood and flesh at that Sun Dance Prayer Ceremony within the chosen land at the Beaver Creek. The Sun Dancers wore breech cloths, front and back, down almost to their ankles. These were held up with deer skin belts. They wore crowns made out of sage and eagle feathers standing up straight on each side of the head.

After that last Sun Dance, five large rocks were rolled down from the top of Beaver Mountain and set at the south end of the Sun Dance Arena. Those rocks were rolled to the fireplace and placed in a V formation with the opening facing directly east. That fireplace had been used only at ceremonial dances. Before and after each dance, the fireplace was used to heat the sweat bath stones. Just west of the fireplace there was a large rock which held the sacrements of the ceremony. The five rocks were left as a memorial to the five warriors who took part, each of whom represented one of the five bands of the Teton Sioux that were present for that occasion.

James Chase In Morning.

That fall scouts came to camp to talk to the chiefs and to have the chiefs talk to Crazy Horse. After reaching a decision, the first chief lit the pipe, then they all smoked it. The last one laid it on the rock.

This pipe which was found in Beaver Valley has lines meaning this: 1st circle—a scalp, 2nd circle—stolen enemy horses, 3rd circle—killing an enemy in battle for the first time, 4th circle—the celebration for the first three events.

In their council, the chiefs decided that Crazy Horse should go in to Fort Robinson. After the council, Crazy Horse rode his horse up to the top of Beaver Mountain, he prayed for guidance for himself. He figured that he was at the end of his trail. He believed something was going to happen. He prophesied that his bones would turn to rock and his joints to flint. Two days later, September 5, 1877, he was killed at Fort Robinson. His body was buried at the place of a steep face rock cliff.

Crazy Horse never wore white man's clothing. He wore buckskin leggings and shirt, and in winter time he added a tanned buffalo robe. Crazy Horse talked to the Sioux Tribe and said, "If I ever pass away, the white men will take you under their custody as wards." *S'ena*— pass away or died; *s'reka*—take into custody. He used these two words, *s'ena s'reka*.

By 1877, many of the people wore government issue clothes, though some still wore buckskin. Mrs. Chase In Morning has a dress that dates back to that time.

The Indians camping in Beaver Valley had the protection of Camp Sheridan from other Indian tribes, if they needed it.

James Chase In Morning says his statement is true, because he is a relative of Crazy Horse. He was related to a sister of Crazy Horse's mother.

JAMES M. CHASE IN MORNING
June 29, 1965

Beaver Creek

In the early 1860s, the Military found the Sioux were already located on Beaver Creek. Red Cloud was new—he was the chief of the Oglala Tribe. Through him they asked the Oglalas about the Brulé Sioux of the east. Then they came to the Beaver Camp to inquire about the tribal people and who was their chief. Iron Shell was their chief, but he appointed Spotted Tail. The army requested where the Indians would make their reservation, whether with the Oglalas or separate. At the time the Brulés decided to settle at Rosebud Creek and call themselves Rosebud Sioux. The Oglalas were asked where they would settle and they decided to go north of the Pine Ridge hills that are north and east of the Beaver Creek area.

Before the territory was ceded to the Government, the Sioux Country extended from the Missouri on the east and north, to the Platte on the south, and to the west past the Black Hills. It was occupied by the seven bands of the Sioux: Lower Brulé or Burnt Thighs, Oglalas, Hunkpapas on Standing Rock, Miniconjou near the river, Blackfoot, Sans Arcs, and Two Kettle.

About 1868, there were two treaties made before government occupation. These were complied with by both the Rosebuds and Oglala Tribes. Before the time of settlement on the Rosebud Reservation, Robinson was a Fort on White River, and Sheridan was a Camp on Beaver Creek.

Beaver Creek was like a permanent or main camping place ever since the Oglalas and Burnt Thighs became acquainted with this area and knew this place. It has never been said which one of the recognized tribes claimed they owned this main camping place. Cultural dances and ceremonial dances were held here. The last genuine worship of the last Sun Dance was held at Beaver Creek.

I have visited this place called Beaver Creek, where several Indians have showed the buttes and places where the chiefs had their camps and where the tipis were placed. There are several places where more historical things were done or did happen, but we noted closely that several burial trees and hills mark the true and faithful place of the Oglalas and Rosebud Brulés and recognized that it was the place chosen by one faithful warrior named Crazy Horse. When he died no person knew or followed when they took his body.

No one ever pointed out the spot where he was buried. Since then no main chief would give clearly in their records that Crazy Horse was buried at any named place.

At a later time Fort Robinson was known as the place where these two nations went and met for their traditional meetings, for by the treaty the surrounding places of hills and creeks were still a part of the Indian country.

The Canadian people to the north were not recognized by the Indians—they were white, but they spoke French. For that reason the Indians had asked the U.S. Military to build forts on the river to prevent stealing by the Canadians or U.S. whites. Now there are no forts on the border.

At this time some whites that are residents of Sheridan County know that Beaver Creek area was the settlement made by these two previously named tribes. Though the entire area of the Dakotas and Nebraska was the birthplace of the Plains Indians, it was in the White River area that they made their treaties to settle on reservations.

In what is now recognized as a county are historical places and sites, and there is a historical part at the place named Beaver Creek. I have visited this place and seen the scenery where my older peoples once settled and lived, and came to be a part of what is called the United States of America.

In those years the Indians never felt homesick, for they knew the country and knew that Beaver Creek was the place where much ceremonial worship was held and where they adopted their U.S. Government which brought the Indians governing rules and which allotted to the Indians land in their own names, on the reservations. Most of which is now heirship land.

HENRY CROW DOG
March 25, 1969

Comments

Told by Henry Crow Dog at his home on Little White River west of Rosebud, South Dakota, April 7, 1967.

In the grass that grew around the springs south of Hay Springs, Nebraska, and toward the Niobrara there was more strength and power, so wild horses gathered there. Alkali was something like salt and the horses liked a little of it.

On Mirage Flats unreal things were visible especially early in mornings. Mirage Flats was like Indian summer—hazy.

The buffalo used to graze over toward Alliance, Nebraska. The buffalo was the main animal in this country before it was settled by white people. At Buffalo Gap, South Dakota the buffalo came out of winter quarters in the spring.

The deer ate bark and oak tips—this gave the deer meat the "wild" taste.

Sitting Bull had dreams, he prophesied. He told the people to stay together. He also prophesied about the killing of the buffalo. Scouts noticed the whites were killing more buffalo than Indians.

Mixed-bloods began to buy hides near the fur traders. Near Laramie Butte they piled their hides, but another whiteman took them. Forts were built to help the whites get buffalo hides, gold, and to drive back the Indians.

White Canadians came to get Indian horses. The Canadians had Canadian Indian scouts.

Crazy Horse knew about the Thunders because he was a Thunder-man. Just as Benjamin Franklin drew electricity from the clouds with a kite and a piece of string, so Crazy Horse received power from the thunders.

He was wise and had understanding like a student who had studied much. At the age of sixteen he went with the warriors. He rode a horse that was a gelding—never a mare or stallion. The gelding reaches its greatest strength at the age of four or five years.

Crazy Horse was not afraid of bears which were the greatest source of danger to man. His horse always warned him of bears or enemies and when Crazy Horse was mounted, the horse rushed off carrying his rider from danger. Because of this, Crazy Horse received his name.

Crazy Horse led in everything on warpaths. He asked the opin-

Henry Crow Dog.

ions of his warriors, but they left it to him, so he directed. He was acquainted in other places. He knew when an attack was to be made on his people. A coyote or a spirit told him.

The Sioux had seven nations. The Tetons were the main chiefs, they had a council on Beaver.

When whites came to Beaver Creek, they sent out scouts to see if there were more Indians back in the hills.

HENRY CROW DOG
March 25, 1969

Last Ride of Chief Crazy Horse

I have now reached the age of 56, living at Pine Ridge, South Dakota. First of all, here is the family history as my grandmother stated to me. Her husband was Chief Fast Thunder, a well-known, noted Indian Scout of the United States Army.

They had four children. The oldest son was given an Indian name (Wicarpi luta) Red Star or Mark Red Star Fast Thunder. Mark had a son, Paul Red Star and a daughter, Stella Swift Bird. The second son, named Luke Plenty Bird, had one daughter, Nancy, his oldest daughter. The third child whose Indian name was (Wakoyake Win) or Fannie Means Fast Thunder. Fannie had three children as follows: Mary (Pacer), Jessie (Eagle Heart), and Theodore Means. The fourth and youngest daughter—Stella King Yellow Shirt had three children: Mathew King, Levi King and Stella King Apple.

My grandmother described Chief Crazy Horse as light complectioned, thin faced, straight nose and he wore braids. (Woman braids). His hair came to his waist.

One day a horseback rider came up from Beaver Creek towards our camp, my grandmother recognized at once that it was Chief Crazy Horse. Upon arrival, Chief Crazy Horse said to Fast Thunder, "Cousin, I finally located you since I had to see you concerning apprehension now at any time." My grandfather requested my grandmother to prepare a mid-day meal so he could eat with his

Jessie Romero Eagle Heart, Matthew Eagle Heart, and Mary Pacer.

cousin (not related, just called each other cousin). While she was preparing the meal she heard them busily talking but she was unable to hear the subject. After they ate, Chief Crazy Horse tied his horse to the team and sat with Fast Thunder in the front seat of the wagon and grandmother sat in back. They drove to Fort Robinson, Nebraska. On arrival at Fort Robinson, they were walking and she was behind them. A guard was walking back and forth by the door as they were about to enter. He looked back and some one stabbed him above his belt on the left side. She heard Chief Crazy Horse saying, "Cousin, you killed me. You are with the white people." He then fell on his face, blood flowing from the wound and he died. My grandmother immediately started singing a brave song for Chief Crazy Horse. She took her blanket and covered him up. His folks were notified at once and they came for his body. They moved him away and to this date no one knows of where he was buried. No one will ever know.

Way afterwards, Fast Thunder moved to the place near Manderson, South Dakota. After his death, grandmother lived in the same house up until she died. She died of old age on January 2, 1934. Before her death some white people from New York came and took her away to someplace, where she was to identify the place where Chief Crazy Horse was killed. Her expenses were all paid. Upon her return from the place, she stated that a record was kept which most of it was wrong.

Upon finding of the peace pipe by Everette White Dress at Mr. Edward T. Kadlecek's residence is a proof of the camp of Fast Thunder where Chief Crazy Horse visited before his death.

JESSIE EAGLE HEART
November 5, 1962

Paper Money

Charles Fire Thunder, who was 75 in 1965, told this story January 1, 1965, at Manderson, S.D. His father, who was 89 when he died in 1937, had told him this story.

Fire Thunder and Crazy Horse were among the warriors that fought the enemies and white soldiers. I will tell about one of the wars in which he and Crazy Horse took part. My father told me just exactly how it happened as he was there and knew all about it. He also told about Crazy Horse's actions in this war. Some Indian warriors went out, my father and Crazy Horse joined them. These Indian warriors sent scouts ahead of them. The scouts returned and told the warriors to hurry and prepare themselves, for soldiers were approaching. They completed their preparations and met the soldiers. The warriors and soldiers took positions on opposite sides of the hill and fought. Finally Crazy Horse went along the soldier's line three times, but they missed him every time. At last the soldiers retreated. The Indian warriors chased them and killed some of them.

Yellow White Man, a Rosebud Sioux, shot a certain soldier off his horse and killed him. He and other warriors stripped this man of his clothing and passed it around. My father was there, but didn't get any of the clothes, however, he was given the soldier's ring.

I am telling this, as I wanted to tell one thing about the soldier. This soldier had on a top-coat when he was killed. This Indian named Yellow White Man took this coat and in it found a long, red pocketbook. It had a number of compartments. In one of them, they found three silver pieces. Later they were told these were silver dollars. At the time they didn't know anything about money. Also in the purse were folded sheets of stiff green paper. They measured about two feet square. The sheets were marked into sections and each section contained a picture of a whiteman. The Indians studied these green papers which they did not understand. Later they learned that these, too, were money. These papers were large sheets of printed United States notes which had not been cut apart. They were probably part of the soldier's payroll. My father said that if Crazy Horse had not scared the soldiers away, they would have received their money.

This man, Yellow White Man, gave the pocketbook to his uncle and said, "Uncle, keep this." This man who received the pocket-

book had a brother-in-law who was a whiteman. The whiteman was
a trader who kept a trading post. His name was Bissonette. His
Indian name was Gray War Bonnet. He was a brother-in-law to my
grandfather. He married my grandfather's cousin. So when the
papers were given to him, he gave each family some of the merchan-
dise he sold or traded. Fire Thunder's family consisted of ten
members, five brothers and five sisters.

Bissonette took these green papers, and for these papers which
the Indians believed were worthless, he gave (so the Indians believed) many things. He gave them dishes, knives, shawls, cloth,
red and blue blankets, guns, and shells for each of the men. These
people thought that Bissonette, the trader, was very generous, but
later as they had more opportunity to become acquainted with green
paper money, they thought they might have given him a very large
sum of money for which things they now knew had no comparable
value.

CHARLES FIRE THUNDER
May 5, 1969

Customs and Beliefs

Written in the Indian language by Charles Fire Thunder in the
winter of 1968-69 and translated by Joe One Feather in February,
1969.

In the days of long ago the Lakota prayed like this. A certain
young maiden brought the peace pipe to a group of people in a
camp. With the peace pipe they are to pray to the Great Spirit.
With this peace you are supposed to pray to the Wakantanka. That is
the way it was handed down from one generation to the other. On a
Sun Dance they prayed with the peace pipe to the Wakantanka.
They selected a ground for the Sun Dance. They prayed there and
do the Sun Dance.

Long time ago when a loved one died the body is placed on a
branch of a tree and watched for 4 days. They dressed the body in
nice skins and place on a branch of a tree. The body is bound in fur

hide and placed on a branch of a tree. The corpse is placed on the tree and never on the ground. The Lakota never camp on one spot. They always travel. After one year of traveling around they come back to the deceased and camp close by. If the bones have fallen down they pick it up and redress it, and place it on a tree again.

All their prayers are honest and straight. They do it right. That is why Lakota are well and happy. What a Lakota wants he prays for and is helped by the Great Spirit. That is the life of the Lakota, there is no more old ways. Now days all our prayers are in vain. Why I say this is the people of this earth have no respect. The Whiteman ruin everything for the Indian. One of these days, the Great Spirit will punish his people. I watch myself on Whiteman's prayer book.

I have some choke cherries. One of these days I will take my peace pipe and pray to the Great Spirit. That is all I want to say.

CHARLES FIRE THUNDER
May 5, 1969

A Time To Remember

My name is Austin Good Voice Flute, now living north of Oglala, South Dakota, reaching the age of 78.

Originally my parents were Cheyenne River Sioux. From there we came to visit the Oglala Sioux. Upon arrival near Pine Ridge, the United States Army met us and made us camp along a small creek now known as Wounded Knee, South Dakota. There they shot us down like some animals. Many were wounded and killed, older people, men, women and children. This happened without warning. My sister and brother were killed there. My mother used to tell me about it. This was very sad and sorrowful because from this many were orphaned and crippled.

My mother's Indian name was "Kuta win," meaning "Lady from Below." She also stated that the Sioux were camping east of Chadron, Nebraska, all along Beaver Creek. There they brought Chief Crazy Horse's body from Fort Robinson, Nebraska, and Chief Crazy Horse's body was left someplace for burial by his parents. Now from what I heard this place is about where Mr. Edward F. Kadlecek lives.

AUSTIN GOOD VOICE FLUTE
February 14, 1963

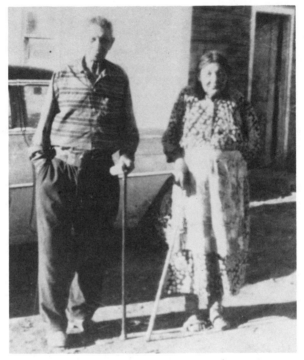

Austin Good Voice Flute and his wife Clara (Chase In
Winter).

Statement

Today, January 8, 1976, I am making this statement at the winter home of the Kadleceks in Alexandria, Louisiana.

I am one-half Osage Indian. I was born in northwest Texas. I lived in the area of Edgemont, South Dakota, for twelve years as I was growing up. I learned to ride horseback while working on ranches there. Later I became acquainted with southwest South Dakota and northwest Nebraska when I had a truck and hauled posts, farm

produce, and lumber from the Black Hills. I return frequently to
that area as I still have friends living there. However, now I make
my home in Alexandria, Louisiana.

This statement is about a story told to me by Chief Stinking Bear
during the County Fair in Edgemont, South Dakota. The year was
1929 or 1930 as I remember. As I am now 64 years and it is hard to go
back all those years and remember things as they really were.

I was visiting my grandmother and I had left my pet coyote tied on
the back porch. When I was ready to leave, I got my pet coyote and
went down the back steps to the sidewalk. I looked up and there
were three Sioux Indians coming down the walk. We reached the
walk almost at the same time and, having respect for my elders, I
stopped to let them pass. The one in the center stopped and asked
me, "By what are you called?" I replied, "My friends call me Little
Herby." He replied, "No, Little Crazy Horse." I noticed this
seemed to upset or shock the other two men. But being a teenage
boy, I gave it very little thought.

Then this man, Stinking Bear, asked me if I would like to visit his
camp that evening. I told him I would come around sundown. Still
bewildered as to why, I took off for home.

Later on that afternoon I walked out to the top of the hill back of or
south of the camp. Then I walked down into the camp. I can't
remember the exact number of wagons and tents in the camp, but as
I got about half way down the camp street, an Indian woman was
cooking something on an open fire and I asked her where Stinking
Bear was. She motioned for me to follow her across the camp street
and stopped in front of a white canvas tent and called. Stinking Bear
came out and motioned for me to come in. The woman said something and he grunted something and she went back to her cooking.

Inside of the tent sitting on the dirt floor was another man. As I
remember his name was American Horse. He was one of the two
with Stinking Bear that I had seen earlier that afternoon. The other
man's name as I remember was Crow Dog. I never saw him but that
one time. Stinking Bear dismissed American Horse and he left.

Stinking Bear asked me if I knew the tale of the War Chief Crazy

Horse. Of course I said no. Well, he told me the story as he was told
of how Crazy Horse lived as he grew up to manhood. Crazy Horse
was a loner, he liked to be by himself. He was a warrior and a
spiritual man.

Stinking Bear told about Crazy Horse being killed and his body
brought back to Beaver Creek and soldiers following who went to
the soldier's camp down the creek.

Then Stinking Bear told of how, unknown to the father and
mother of Crazy Horse, he had followed them out of the camp when
they took their son's body off on a travois. He had watched when
they buried Crazy Horse. Crazy Horse, still wrapped in the buffalo
hide, was placed, standing up, in a crevice or crack in a bluff. Then
they pried and dug with sticks and started a big slide of rocks that
completely covered him.

After they came back the father went into his tipi. The mother
went to a hillside and sat down on a rock. Stinking Bear went to his
own folks' tipi and sat beside it where he could watch the old woman
doing the death chant. He watched her the rest of the night. She sat
where she could see the three black pinnacles along the wall. They

Lawson R. Gregg.

were black in the moonlight. They were the marker for her son's grave. All night long she sat there singing the death chant or smoking a pipe. When morning came she laid the pipe there on a rock.

Stinking Bear told me not one tale but a number of them. They all sounded real to me. But by two or three days I had put them out of my mind and had gone my own way. So I never really knew why he called me Little Crazy Horse.

Some forty-five years later, some Indians doing a Show of Dances in Alexandria told me it was because of the coyote. They said that Crazy Horse himself had a coyote that followed him like a dog.

So in 1975, I went to Nebraska and from the tales told to me, I pointed out where the body of Crazy Horse is or where I believe it is. The place is on the right side of the Beaver Creek Road (going northwest) below three mounds or pinnacles about one-half mile from where the Beaver Creek Camp was located on now Eddie Kadlecek property.

My Vision

Visions are hard to understand but can be very real. I was riding south and east out of Edgemont, South Dakota toward the Black Hills. As I started up the first little shale grade up into the hills some kind of instinct kept telling me to turn around and look behind me. At the top of the grade I turned my horse and looked back toward Edgemont. I then turned my head left and looked toward the washed out or cut banks.

I saw a band of Indians on small horses ride out of a fog. I saw this band or family with a small girl standing on a travois with her hand on the horse's hip. She was wearing a buckskin skirt. I didn't see very much as shortly they rode into another fog. This small band of Indians came out of one fog and went into another fog on a bright sunshiny day. I don't know if this was a dream or what, but I was scared.

L. R. GREGG
January 13, 1976

Dora High Whiteman.

Statement

My Indian name is Gli Nan Jin Win, Dora High Whiteman, age 80, Post Office, Oglala, South Dakota. My parents are from Cheyenne River, South Dakota. We came to visit the Oglala Sioux's before arrival at Pine Ridge. The United States soldiers made us camp at a place. This place now known as Wounded Knee, South Dakota. I was ten years old at the time of this massacre. It was a terrible sight to see.

I married Mr. Grant High Whiteman and we made our home here along the White River, west of Oglala, South Dakota. Lived here ever since. My husband is a religious person. He takes part in all activities. He was highly respected and he served as one of the judges of the Oglala Sioux Tribe for several years.

My neighbor, Mrs. Edna No Fat, died of old age several years ago: While she was living, we used to talk about what was going on years ago. She mentioned about a Sun Dance, which was held along Beaver Creek, east of Chadron, Nebr. She was riding a horse, watching the dance and all of a sudden some one shot in her face, made her horse jump. She said she didn't fall off the horse and here it was her boy friend, whom she broke away from. That was the punishment for her for her unhappy boy friend. She stated the Rosebud Sioux's also used the camp all along the Beaver Creek. Of course, unable to point at the exact place. Anyway, near this place, there is a place called marker hill, where two hills are kind of close together.

DORA HIGH WHITEMAN
November 14, 1963

Making Ready for Civilization by Chief Crazy Horse

History as told by Chief Iron Shell, Hollow Horn Bear of Rosebud Sioux by Mrs. Julia Hollow Horn Bear, Rosebud Sioux of Parmelee, South Dakota.

Just before the Rosebud Sioux made their settlement here at the Rosebud Indian Reservation they were living along Beaver Creek, east and north of Chadron, Nebraska. Chief Iron Shell related to Chief Crazy Horse, know the reason of why Chief Crazy Horse was killed. As told his last words he spoke, I hold no ill will against any of them although some who I believed to be my friends have betrayed me after all this all fair in this world for life here is just a gamble, you either lose or win and I happen to be one of the unfortunates, I waged war to preserve our rights but lost. We are a conquered race. It is rather hard for me to say at this time of how he was killed. If Chief Crazy Horse was living he could have had a better understanding between the Government and the Indians. Chief Crazy Horse's body was brought back to the camp at Beaver Creek, followed by white people trying to steal the body. One of my aunts cleaned the body of Chief Crazy Horse.

Parents of Chief Crazy Horse moved away before sunrise. No one knows where they buried their son. Only thing I know today is that Beaver Creek, Beaver Walls, the chosen land of Chief Crazy Horse, where a sparkling stream flow very gently supply with plenty of fish, beavers, etc., the forest walls and the valleys where there is plenty of wild fruit, the place where deer and buffaloes also love to graze.

While camping along Beaver Creek, grandfather (Brown Cap), his name is given him because he is a trapper. His cap was made from beaver skin. One day while he went to check his traps to see if he had any catch, which he didn't. As he was pulling his catch to the shore and unloosing it, someone from behind said, Hey. I am your friend let your catch free and go home with me as I wanted to talk to you because you will be my friend. He then left everything he had at the place, peace pipe, etc., and started following him. They came to a door, went inside, found some people inside they gave him a place to sit by the table they talk for a long time, he did not return home for two or three days. The people began worrying of him not returning home. Just then he returned home. As people gather about, glad to see him, he started telling of his experience that he met some white people inviting him to visit their home. Upon arrival at their home they had a table where he sat with them talking. He was told that his people will soon live with white people and talk their language and that he must tell his people to try to be real friends, associate and cooperate with them. He also brought gifts, a cross made with willow branches, a notebook with writing on it for him to read and a pencil. By the cross the Indian will be converted that this is a symbol of almighty God. They will believe that there is a God. The notebook they showed him taught him to read, etc., also taught him the use of the pencil. They went on saying in two days from now more white people will be moving in on the Indian territory, traveling in covered wagons. They also taught him how to speak the white man's language, the names, etc. On the day the white people arrived in covered wagons, grandpa went to talk to them. He held his arm out meaning "welcome friends." Introducing himself as Baptiste Good, the name what was given him. He talked to these people. He understood and spoke very well of their language. They were more than happy to talk to him. They gave him food, etc. Now, that the white people that taught grandpa all this, were beavers that lived along Beaver Creek.

Grandpa Baptist Good, first Indian that used a white man's name, also named his relatives as follows, the names still carried by the descendants: Patrick High Hawk, Joseph Good, Bernard Grabbing Bear, Zona One Bear, Emma Blue Bird, Beatrice White Feather and Gertie Sweat House. The Indians were amazed at these names.

Chief Crazy Horse, an honest man, who defends his people, protects their land, the Black Hills, etc., was feared by the Indians and white people.

Now the notebook was the beginning of writing. In the beginning, the keeping of records was done by simple kind of writing, which was called picture drawing. This same notebook given to my

Julia and Dan Hollow Horn Bear.

grandfather is being kept at Rapid City, South Dakota. I will get it back to be displayed soon. You can imagine of all these happenings of how Indians' earliest discoveries were. The Beaver Creek now look different from the way it did at that time. There were no buildings, no roads, no fields, no fences, everywhere were dark forests or plains of grass. Animals moved about through them, searching for food. This was the chosen land of Chief Crazy Horse. The notebook is the evidence we still have that was given us to use by beavers from the Beaver Creek.

JULIA HOLLOW HORN BEAR
January 4, 1963

History of Old Chiefs

Mita Kola pi
My Friends
   Chief Iron Shell was one of the Head Chiefs of the Brulé Sioux Nation. He was one of the signers of the 1868 Treaty. His thumb print is in the 1868 Treaty Law Books which are in the Rosebud Indian Office. In 1872, Agent Maj. D. R. Risley gave Iron Shell a recommendation stating that "his disposition is good towards the Government and all the whites and his efforts to maintain peace and quietness amongst his tribe is worthy of every encouragement and consideration." The recommendation was dated July 10, 1872, Whetstone Agency, White River, D.T. [Dakota Territory]. The original copy is now in possession of Carl Iron Shell, Rosebud, South Dakota.
   Grandfather Chief Iron Shell had seven wives. They were all sisters and cousins. This was before the 1868 Treaty was made.
   One of his sons was named Iron Shell after his father. Maj. Gen. George Crook, called Three Star by the Indians, stated in a safe conduct permit issued to his son, that he "is an intelligent Indian and desirous of becoming a self supporting, self respecting citizen. I bespeak for him the act of friendship of every friend of the Indian." The original paper was signed June 9, 1889, by George Crook, Maj.

Gen. U.S.A. from Headquarters Division of the Missouri. This original paper is in the possession of Carl Iron Shell of Rosebud, South Dakota.

Another son of Iron Shell was Chief Hollow Horn Bear. He was a very intelligent Indian and friendly to every white man in the United States. When Woodrow Wilson was president of the United States, Chief Hollow Horn Bear was a delegate to Washington, D.C. He was a delegate with honorable intentions. He died there in Washington in 1913.

From Chief Iron Shell's generation up to this day there were six generations and some of the generations have become mixed white people. It is a very big generation now days.

My father, Peter Iron Shell, told of the Chief Iron Shell generation. He said that Chief Two Strike, Chief He Dog, Chief Turning Bear, and Chief Crazy Horse were all big chiefs who had, at one time, all been in Beaver Valley. He also said that Chief Iron Shell and Chief Crow Dog were cousins.

The Killing of Spotted Tail

While Chief Crow Dog was chief of police at Rosebud, the Government issued him a wagon. One day a wheel tire on his wagon became loose, so Crow Dog took his wagon wheel over to the Rosebud Agency to the blacksmith worker and told him to fix this wagon wheel for him. While waiting, Crow Dog took his police officers with him to check up on the Reservation border line.

They were on the west side of the river and when they had gone about half way towards the east, they came to a ranch. This rancher was a white man and he had about a thousand head of cattle enjoying free grazing. As Crow Dog and his officers stopped there they watched a white cowboy coming toward them. He was driving a buggy hitched to a sorrel team and tied to the side of the team was a saddle horse with a saddle. Crow Dog asked the white cowboy for payment for the free grazing of his cattle. The cowboy said, "I paid to Spotted Tail already so I can't make two payments. Spotted Tail gave me a permit to graze this cattle in his country."

Crow Dog said to his officer, "Go and untie the saddle horse at the side of the team and get that fur overcoat which the cowboy has in his buggy." So the policeman took the saddle horse and the saddle overcoat. Then Crow Dog said to go and kill one of the cattle and his men butchered the animal. The men stayed two or three days and then went back to the reservation headquarters to report that Spotted Tail had stolen Tribal money. But the superintendent only said, "He is Chief."

After he finished his work he went to his blacksmith worker to find out if the wagon wheel was finished. But the wheel had not been worked on. Crow Dog said, "Why didn't you work on my wagon wheel?"

The blacksmith worker said that Chief Spotted Tail told him not to fix it, "So that's why I didn't work on it," he said.

Crow Dog went to meet Spotted Tail in front of the office. They had an argument there. Spotted Tail said, "First time if I see you some place, I'll kill you."

Crow Dog answered, "I never wish nothing in my life. If I want to do some bad or good, I go and do it. That's the kind of man I am."

Well, at about the same time, Chief Spotted Tail had taken away another man's wife. The man's name was Chief Hind Leg.

Spotted Tail went to the Pine Ridge Reservation. After he came back he was to go to Washington, D.C. on tribal business. He was going to appoint some chiefs, but before he made the appointments, the chiefs told him to give back to Hind Leg, his wife. Chief Spotted Tail said, "No, I am going to take my new wife along to show the officer at Washington D.C." At this he dismissed the council and the other chiefs were sad.

Chief Spotted Tail started going back to his place. He rode bareback. About half way there, Crow Dog and his wife were coming to his wagon. Crow Dog got off the wagon, took his old timer gun and set back of his wagon. Spotted Tail came near to him so Crow Dog pulled his gun on him. He shot him on the side of his body and the bullet went out of Spotted Tail's right shoulder. Spotted Tail fell off the horse.

About this time Chief He Dog and Two Strike met Crow Dog and tried to take away his gun. They couldn't do it, so they let him go. Crow Dog unhitched one of his horses, he got on the horse and went home and his wife followed him back home.

The police took Crow Dog to Deadwood, South Dakota, to jail. But at that time there was only one law between white and Indians. If Indian kill white man, this Indian gave in to the white men. That's all the law they had on those days. Chief Crow Dog served some time in the Deadwood jail and he was released from jail to come back to the Rosebud Reservation.

How Spotted Tail Became Chief

Spotted Tail received his name from a white man, because he wore a coonhide cap with a tail on it that was given him by a white man.

There was a mail route west from the Missouri River. Spotted Tail and some other young warriors stopped a wagon and killed the driver. The white police officers wanted the warriors who had done it. They said they were going to take the warriors and teach them what was right, because they had killed a mail carrier and taken all his goods, money, and everything. The chiefs said that the warriors should go with the white officers. Iron Shell told Spotted Tail that if he came back safe, he could have Iron Shell's shawl and would be made a chief. After a stay in prison, Spotted Tail did return safely and he received his title of chief.

Before 1868 Treaty, the Sioux Nation lived without law. They were against the white people and other tribes of Indians. Once when white people attacked the Sioux nation the members fled from the white people. Some of the Indian squaw women got caught. These squaw women surrendered to the white people. After while they were released from the white people and they all came back pregnant. Some of the squaw women disappeared. From what happened some of this mixed blood Indians were raised.

Chief Crazy Horse

When Custer lost his battle Crazy Horse was there. Custer was wiped out clean along with many of the United States Troops. After the battle was over, there was only one cavalry man let go. The Sioux people said to each other, "Let him go, let him go." He was going to take a message back to the white people. The pockets of Custer's troops were searched and silver and paper money were found. After while my grandfather realized it was money.

Crazy Horse was one of the chiefs who had been in Beaver Valley. He got power from the Thunders. He dreamed about the Thunders and he talked to those Thunders. Chief Crazy Horse was a brave man.

CARL IRON SHELL, JR.
May 13, 1969

Frank Kicking Bear and Charles Fire Thunder.

A Talk by Two Friends

My name is Frank Kicking Bear of Manderson, S. D. I am now 75 years old. I will tell briefly what I have learned from my father about Chief Crazy Horse. When he was 14 years old he received the Holy Message on the top of a hill now called Scottsbluff, and since, he took part in many great wars with white soldiers and enemy from other tribes of Indians. He carried a small stone on his person. It was a sacred stone. Everybody in those days knew this. Just before the war started he rubbed this stone all over his body. Then he took dirt from a gopher hill and sprinkled it all over his body. This made him bullet or arrow proof. He was a great leader of his warriors until he got killed.

I am Charles Fire Thunder of Manderson, S. D. I am now 72 years old. Of course, Crazy Horse died long time ago, but I will tell something about his life which my father told me. Since Crazy Horse was 17 years old, he was a great fighter in the war with white soldiers and enemy and other tribes and he was a well experienced man. I am only telling a small part of his story. My father told me, also that he carried a small stone, just before a war started he rubbed all over his body with the stone, also his horse, also sprinkled himself with dirt from gopher hills to make himself weapon proof. After the white soldiers found out all about him, they offered a treaty, but instead of peace he met death. He is well remembered by all of his descendents. Now today there are none of us who possesses the talent he had in those days. He had a great talent. He was protecting our people and land, that someday his people might live in peace upon this land. Well, in early days the different tribes of Indians were fighting each other in wars. One year there was a war between the Sioux and the Crows. They were fighting all day. It was a hard fight, finally, Crazy Horse got on his horse and took charge all alone. Of course, the enemy's weapons did not bother him at all. So the enemy had to retreat. The enemy headed for a deep canyon and took a stand there, but the Crazy Horse warriors won the battle.

Crazy Horse was a leader of the warriors who fought General Custer. There were only twenty-five warriors at the start of this battle. Gradually other warriors came in to take part as the battle went on. Once in a while Crazy Horse would expose himself to the soldiers, so they could take a good aim and shoot at him. Finally the warriors wiped out Custer and his men. After the battle was won the Indians had a big Victory Dance. After the dance, the young warriors wore soldiers' uniforms and had a parade with Crazy Horse in the lead. One certain warrior took the bugle and blew the instrument in any way that he could. These young warriors in uniforms marched and imitated the soldiers drilling, and they were pretty good, so other people were wondering where they learned all of this. There were hundreds of white soldiers who were killed. The news spread all over. Custer and his men were completely wiped out in less than a day. The reason was, Crazy Horse was the commander of these warriors that fought Custer. On account of Crazy Horse, white soldiers or enemies could not take advantage of his people. He was a courageous man, for he knew himself that in war there was no weapon that would harm him.

Frank Kicking Bear: I will tell a short story about the Sun Dance. My grandfather, his name was Chagla, was the founder of the Sun Dance. He went to the Black Hills one time. As he went about the hills, he heard a dream and he followed the dream sound. As he went around, he saw all kinds of deer and elk were dancing in a circle, and after the dance they paired up and went back in the hills. This was where he learned all the Sun Dance songs. He saw that in the form of humans. This was the beginning of the Sun Dance. Through this Sun Dance they worship the Great Spirit, and it is the greatest religious gathering the Indians ever had.

Charles Fire Thunder: The Indians used to have a way of worshipping the Great Spirit. Whenever they had a problem confronting them, for instance, sickness or trouble of any kind, they offered themselves to dance. They were pierced and they danced for three or four days without food and water, and had no sleep. They offered prayers to the Great Spirit, and their prayers were answered. Therefore, the Indians considered this the greatest religious gathering among them in those days.

Frank Kicking Bear: I will tell you a short story about my grandfather, Chagla, who knew all about the Horse Dance. He was a founder of the Horse Dance, also. The people in those days usually got together in the summer time. When they had this Horse Dance, they had a song for this ceremony. I will sing the song later in this statement. The Indians had the Horse Dance annually, the same as the Sun Dance. The reason for the Horse Dance was to raise more useful horses and to increase the herds so they might have enough good horses to hunt buffalo or with which to fight their enemies.

The following are the words of a Horse Dance Song:

Watch the horses are come dancing
Watch the horses are come dancing
Watch the horses are come dancing
Watch closely a herd of black horses come dancing.

Black horses represented west, white horses represented north, buckskin represented east, gray horses represented south.

Charles Fire Thunder: I will add a little more about what we have told about Crazy Horse as a great warrior and leader. Now as we have already stated, he wore a little, round, mysterious rock, he also had on his person a little medicine bag. Just before each battle he would chew a small portion of this medicine and rub it on his body. Then he sprinkled his body with dirt from gopher hills. Then he picked out a tall grass stem and stuck the same in his hair. Then he blew on his Indian bone-whistle and circled around the white soldiers or Indian enemies from other tribes. They would take shots at him, but fail to hit him. He was well known all over the country, that is, white people and Indians knew about his talent and bravery.

Frank Kicking Bear: I will tell some more about Crazy Horse. Rosebuds were camping here and Crazy Horse's cousin, this man's name was Fast Thunder. They both went to Fort Robinson. As they arrived Crazy Horse was taken into custody, and when he refused, a soldier stabbed him, but he did not die instantly, but lived awhile and finally he died. I will tell this much about Crazy Horse.

Charles Fire Thunder: Concerning the statements we have given in regard to Crazy Horse's actions, Kicking Bear was a member of Chief Crazy Horse's band and also associated with him. Therefore what we have told about Crazy Horse is true. We did not intend to tell anything that's untrue. Therefore in the future anyone who reads or hears this statement, that person should be satisfied that it is true.

Kicking Bear, 1896, by William Dinwiddie. (*Smithsonian Institution National Anthropological Archives*)

Frank Kicking Bear: I will tell briefly about the Ghost Dance. Kicking Bear performed a Ghost Dance Ceremony, but first Kicking Bear and some other man went to see a man. This man gave them instructions concerning the Ghost Dance and they performed the Ghost Dance. My grandfather had what they called sacred paint. If he painted anyone with the sacred paint, he knows everything beyond a person's knowledge. To this day I still have the sacred paint that they used. As I understood, to this day, they were trying to teach our people religion, so they added the Ghost Dance to what they taught them. This is what I believe.

Charles Fire Thunder: I will tell something about the Indian worship. They had the Sun Dance Ceremony every year about mid-summer. In this ceremony they had several ways of worshipping the Great Spirit. Today I have seen an old Sun Dance ground and was wondering. On this ground I have observed they laid some stones. As I have seen, these stones represented each band of Indians that participated in this Sun Dance. They have but five stones towards the south. That shows that five different bands of Indians took part.

Frank Kicking Bear: South of Mr. Edward Kadlecek's place there is a high pointed hill. Upon that hill back in 1942, Black Crow fasted for three days and nights. He told his main purpose of fasting. He prayed that the Indian generations may be increased and live a better life; that there is peace among nations, and that more crops and whatever they possess will be taken care of. This was his prayer.

Charles Fire Thunder: We have talked about Crazy Horse's life in connection with his actions in the battles at different times. We have learned this from Kicking Bear and Fire Thunder [fathers] as they associated with Crazy Horse. Crazy Horse always followed his own mind. One day his two cousins came to him and requested that he grant them two sacred, tanned colt hides. They wore these hides when in battle and, of course, they were not as good as Crazy Horse, but they could avoid getting hit. What we have told about his word and deed are true.

Frank Kicking Bear: In regard to the Ghost Dance, they had a

certain song to open the dance with. I will now sing that song:
>   Everything grows on the earth are ours
>   My father said.
> Second Song:
>   Here comes someone looking for his mother.
>   (repeat three times)

Charles Fire Thunder: I will tell a short story about what my grandfather told me. His name was Good Hawk. "Grandson, in early days the Rosebud people had the bad cases of cramps, not all, but part of the people and children. There were considerable numbers of people and children who died. They didn't know of any medicine that would cure them, but they were treated with heat. Maybe that helped. We thought the Indians were getting help from the Great Spirit, but we got punishment instead." Grandfather told me again, "Grandson, one time the people were afflicted with sores, they itched all over the body, but they had medicine to cure that, so they helped each other. The medicine helped some, others, not much. They offered prayers that they might not have another sickness or disease inflicted on them, and later they thought that they contracted the sickness and diseases from the clothes and food given to them, which was imported. Therefore they gathered all the clothing and made a big fire and burned them. They went back to buckskin clothes again. They also prayed that there would not be any more sickness or diseases come to them. After that a woman with a little girl came close where the Rosebuds were camping, and the woman laid her baggage on the ground and lay down and failed to get up. So they went to her. A man said that she might be dead. "I will go and see if she is dead. I will take the girl around and save her." So he went and found the woman dead. He picked up the girl and took her and saved her. All the people saw this.

Frank Kicking Bear: I want you to listen to this. Sixty years ago there was a certain cattleman ranching in the state of Idaho. One day this rancher disappeared. They searched for him, but failed to find him. So one day a man put on buckskin clothes and carrying a gun and blanket over his back went to look for him. Soon a cloud covered him, and that was the last thing he remembered. When he came to, he found himself in a huge nest. There were two young buzzards sitting in the nest. Also there was the missing rancher and his horse. Some other people were laying there, too. Some skeletons were scattered around. The huge buzzard was sitting nearby. He took careful aim, shot it in the head, and killed it. The big bird or buzzard went down. He fed the little ones meat and he ate some of the meat. As soon as the little ones were big enough to fly, he tied ropes around their legs, so they helped him land. He landed on top of a pine tree. He found the dead buzzard in a canyon nearby, its tail feathers were about thirty-five feet long. This was not an eagle, it was altogether a different kind of buzzard. So, in spite of the smell from the spoiled bird, he pulled this tail feather. Afterwards he shot the little ones.

[This statement is a copy of a conversation made on tape by Frank Kicking Bear and Charles Fire Thunder at the home of Edward Kadlecek, on Beaver Creek, north of Hay Springs, Nebraska, in the summer of 1963. The tape recording is in the Sioux language. It was translated into English by Joe White Face on July 12, 1966. Frank Kicking Bear died as the result of a car accident, so this translation of their conversation is signed only by Charles Fire Thunder.]

CHARLES FIRE THUNDER
May 5, 1969

Life of Crazy Horse and Fast Thunder

My name is Mathew H. King. I am a full-blooded Indian, a member of the Oglala Sioux Tribe of the Pine Ridge Oglala Sioux Indian Reservation, Pine Ridge, South Dakota, and am presently residing in Scottsbluff, Nebraska.

The following recording and narration of the Life of Crazy Horse and Fast Thunder was made at Mr. and Mrs. Edward Kadlecek's residence, Chadron, Nebraska, Sunday, March 12, 1967.

I became interested in Indian stories and histories at a very early age. What I have written here was written to the best of my knowledge, as it was related to me by persons or warriors who were there. Crazy Horse and Fast Thunder were very closely related. Together they fought in many battles against other tribes. They fought and defeated the United States armies. They defeated Fetterman, Crook, and Custer. I am sure every human on the face of the earth wants to be free. Crazy Horse was no exception, for freedom was his life before the coming of the whitemen. He wanted to continue to live a free life to the end of his days. He did not want to be placed in a fenced reservation. He loved his country. He loved what he found in it, and he enjoyed it. He believed in absolute freedom with no laws to govern one's life except natural laws. He preferred to die protecting that belief rather than to be enslaved in a whiteman's cell, for imprisonment is contrary to the freedom which the Great Spirit has given to his children, the Red Race.

Crazy Horse was camping at the mouth of Rosebud Creek near Lame Deer, Montana, when the government thought that if Crazy Horse was brought in, the life and changes of the Sioux would be complete. So the government sent a delegation of Sioux to bring him in. It failed. Another group was sent and it also failed. Now the third group that went out, was composed of dog soldiers, and his own relatives, including Chief Fast Thunder who was an Indian scout for the United States Army at the time. This group went to Montana and had a conference with Crazy Horse, but Crazy Horse did not want to come in. His distrust of the whitemen was greater than the promises made by that group. He saw where liquor and disease brought by the white people to the Indian people destroyed the Indian race. He said the civilization of the white and the civilization of the Indian was just as far apart as the sun and the moon. They could not work together because they had different genealogies. Their ethics in life were very different. So Crazy Horse refused to come. The delegation then worked on Crazy Horse's father and mother to induce Crazy Horse to come in. Before this group had left Fort Robinson, they were instructed that if Crazy Horse came back to Fort Robinson, all his promises and all his wishes would be provided for and secure the rest of their days.

Those were some of the promises made to Crazy Horse through Chief Fast Thunder and this group that went to Montana. After several days of conference, Crazy Horse finally consented. But even after he had consented, he still didn't believe a word that was promised, even though it had been said by some of the great warriors—Sioux warriors that had come after him.

You know I have been informed by other warriors who were closely associated with Crazy Horse that when he left Rosebud Creek, he was heard to say, "All is lost anyway. Because most of the Sioux people are running for shelter in the opposite direction, the country is lost. The country, the civilization the Indian enjoyed, and the freedom is lost." Still he was willing to go, no matter what happened. Some of the warriors said that he knew that he was going to a fate; that the worst tragedy was waiting for him at the other end. But this he didn't care, for he gave himself up, all the way through—according to the people who were closely associated with him. He joined the group and came to Fort Robinson. After there awhile, he realized that some of his own people, through the whiteman, had betrayed him. In fact, in these modern times we realize that the leaders of the Sioux and the leaders of the United States Army fooled the people of the Sioux and also some of the army men. Misinformation was given to this group.

Crazy Horse was taken to jail instead of a conference table. He stopped; he told the people that were taking him there, "You are taking me to jail." He started to back up and one of the guards stuck him through the kidney on the right side above the hip with a bayonet. He was wounded and died that same night.

Chief Fast Thunder, who was instructed and was ordered and had promised to take Crazy Horse in, was shocked. He didn't believe what he saw. He got into trouble with the commanders. He got mad. If he had had his own way, and if there hadn't been so many peace makers there at the time, there would have erupted a war between the Sioux and the soldiers at the fort. Instead, he left the fort and camped someplace in the hills between what is now Hay Springs and Chadron, to cool down. There his boys or his followers were with him. They smoked the peace pipe and discussed the tragedy of their leader. They didn't know what to do, for if some of the heads of the greatest government in the world lied, who could be trusted.

At the time when Crazy Horse was a great warrior, there were three different things which were most important to Indian life. That was to be a great warrior, a great scout, or a great hunter. Usually the three did not go together, a man must be a master of one—that is, excell in only one of them. But Crazy Horse and High Breast were equal in all of these occasions, according to the history that had been handed down by the Sioux. High Breast and Crazy Horse were two of the greatest of all great Sioux warriors.

Chief Sitting Bull who was elected by the Sioux Indians at large was the only Indian-made chief at that time. He was recognized as an official chief of the Sioux Nation, for he was selected by the council of the Sioux. We have had many chiefs since that time, but many were made chief because they favored the whiteman. They were whiteman-made chiefs, so the Indians did not look at them as chiefs since they were not selected by the members of the Sioux Nation.

Crazy Horse was elected chief and was given a shirt and a war-bonnet. After wearing the shirt for awhile he returned it. At the council he said, "I'd rather be a plain warrior. I'm not an orator, I'm not a politician," (in this modern way of speaking) so he returned the war-shirt, and he was a warrior until his end.

I will tell a few of the experiences that Crazy Horse had. As a young man he had a dream that he would receive his powers from the Thunder Gods. He continued to have this dream time and time again, so he believed in it. He believed in this during all of his life. He put his whole faith in this thing which gave him a power to use—the power for his protection, and the power to protect his own people. He made this prophecy, "If anything happens to me, I will return to the Thunder Gods and from there I will look after my people with the power of the Thunder Gods." This power protected him in the wars against the Shoshones, or Snakes, the Blackfeet, the

Flatheads, the Crows, the Ree, the Pawnees, and many different tribes. When I mentioned something about the history of other tribes, I missed the Cheyenne Indians. However, the Cheyenne Indians were closely related or allied with the Sioux. In fact, the relation was so close that there were many inter-marriages. There were many half-Cheyenne and half-Sioux in the two tribes.

While Crazy Horse was a very young man, he became associated with High Breast, one of the greatest Sioux warriors at the time, as was stated by the Sioux warriors in later years. High Breast received his name because he was so muscular, his chest was huge. He has also been called Hump. We all know that High Breast, or Hump, was killed in war in 1871 by the Shoshones. He was a teacher to Crazy Horse and there was a friendly rivalry between the two. They always competed to see which one could kill the most enemies and which one could take the most scalps. This was all in friendly gesture, but nevertheless, it was true. This I learned from some of the warriors.

Crazy Horse met and fought, including the United States Army and defeating them, some of the most learned strategists of the United States Army, General Crook, General Miles, General Custer, and Lt. Col. Fetterman. Crazy Horse was the general and commander-in-chief in all of these battles. He was a strategist. He laid out the plans of attack, he laid out the plans on how they could defeat the enemies. All the Indians depended on him. During the Custer Battle the Indians estimated that some 850 to 1150 men were attacking the camps. Crazy Horse on the night before the battle instructed his warriors that there would be many soldiers in that valley the next morning, but he said, "The Great Spirit has already told me, we're going to win this war, so be not afraid, but go out there and fight." And he added, "You cowards lay back, the Great Spirit gave us every day a beautiful day to die in." That day Custer met his fate.

I learned the following from the Cheyenne warriors. One of them who fought in that war told me that while they were waiting, he turned around. Someone told him that Crazy Horse was coming, so he turned and saw him. Crazy Horse who was the last one to leave the camp was heading toward where the warriors—the Cheyenne and the Sioux—congregated together for the attack. The soldiers were upon a ridge. The warriors didn't know what to do; they were waiting for Crazy Horse. When this warrior saw Crazy Horse coming, he told the other Cheyennes to be ready, "for Crazy Horse will never stop, he will attack and we must attack."

Instead of that, Crazy Horse told them to wait. He went toward the hill and rode in front of the soldier's line of fire. The smoke from the guns of the soldiers made a smoke screen. We all know that black powder was used in the guns at that time and it made a lot of smoke. Then he turned and went back the same way and they put up another smoke screen. He went back to his warriors, for it was now time to attack. Many soldiers met their fate that day including a lot of Indian scouts. There were 25 to 30 some odd Indian scouts killed in that war with Custer. Some of this has never been revealed because the Indians were threatened that if they had a 45-70 or a 45-90 gun, they would be arrested. So grandfather told me that after Custer was wiped out, one soldier escaped and he was three or four miles away from the battle when the warriors asked, "Shall we get him?"

"No," one of the warriors said, "leave him to tell the story."

Well, when the soldier saw some warriors on the top of the hill, he got off his horse and shot himself. So he didn't tell the story.

Crazy Horse fought General Crook at the head of the Rosebud Creek and defeated him. Chief Plenty-Coup who was a Crow scout at the time told a complete history of this battle and probably later I will tell in detail some of these battles which had taken place and which was told by the Indians who took part in it and not by white historians. The only things I can rely on from some of these historians are the dates, actually the date an event occurred, but as far as the fighting is concerned, I want to get it from the Indian's standpoint of the history and his viewpoint.

Many historians have written that in the Custer Battle, the Sioux, Cheyennes and Arapahoes took part; this is untrue. The warriors who fought Custer were Sioux and Cheyenne. There were only four Arapahoes, and I learned this from the Arapahoes themselves. I'm going to record it here. It seems that four Arapahoes got into the Sioux Camp just after the General Crook and Crazy Horse fight at the head of Rosebud Creek. That was just about a week or ten days before Custer's battle. The Sioux caught these four Arapahoes. Thinking they were scouts for the United States Army, they were going to kill them. They tied the prisoners up to a post and were ready to kill them when Chief Sitting Bull interfered. He told them by sign language that there would be a fight in a few days. "If you put on your war shirts and fight with us then you live, and if you don't," he said, "you'll die, you will die in the same manner that the white soldiers will die in a few days." Now this was some of the prophecy of Chief Sitting Bull.

Of course, later, I found out that the southern tribes had sent runners to the northern tribes to tell of the activities of General Custer in the south. The messengers told that "there's a man with long hair killing small tribes—men, women and children—and taking prisoners in the south and now he's heading this way."

But Sitting Bull had received a message long before, and it was never revealed by any historians. He instructed his people to congregate at the Little Big Horn for a meeting where they had an annual Sun Dance and prayed to the Great Spirit.

So the Arapahoes escaped death and took part in Custer's battle. They bragged about how they whipped Custer, but the other Arapahoes didn't believe them. But it was true that these four Arapahoes fought with the Sioux in Custer's battle along the Little Big Horn River.

After the peace was made Fast Thunder settled down between Manderson and Wounded Knee, South Dakota, and the government helped him. He became one of the well-to-do Indians of his time. He had many workers, in fact, he had two whitemen working for him. He had many ponies and cattle.

As a very young man, I was very close to Chief Fast Thunder and on many occasions I heard his remark, "They fooled me!" He carried a 45-70 gun with him at all times. He would be sitting along the bank of Wounded Knee Creek gazing into the valley and along the hills and every once in awhile he would say, "They fooled me!" I can imagine what went through his mind as he made these remarks. The days of Crazy Horse were in his memories and the days—or times—when great leaders lied to other leaders, even though they represented the Great Spirit (missionaries or church people who made treaties) and smoked the peace pipe, but that was not the life of our American Indian. The peace pipe was a religion—a go between—between the Great Spirit and themselves. So when they lit the pipe they prayed and then smoked and knew they must never tell a lie. So what goes through Fast Thunder's mind at the time was true and was something that was power before the Great Spirit. It was something that the whiteman does not understand. Those were some of the things which happened in 1877 at Fort Robinson, Nebraska.

MATHEW H. KING
April 14, 1970

Chief Crazy Horse's Last Stop

I am now 69 years old and live in Pine Ridge, South Dakota. My Grandfather, on my Mother's side, was Fast Thunder, a chief of the Oglala Sioux. Grandfather was also an Indian Scout for the United States Army.

Mother's name was Sag ye—meaning "Cane" and she was also known by the name of Tasunke opi or "Wounded Horse." Mother told me the Oglala Sioux and the Rosebud Sioux used to camp along the valleys of White Clay Creek and other creeks near the Pine Ridge Reservation.

The Rosebud Sioux Issue Station was located in the vicinity of what is now known as the Comer place and the Oglala Sioux Issue Station was located near the Greenwood place.

The Indians would camp in groups and as a rule did not raise large families. In those days, most families would have two and three children and were always prepared to vacate a camp area and start traveling. Because the Army was stationed among the Indians, some families would slip away to another location.

The Rosebud Sioux used to camp near the spot where Beaver Creek flows into White River. Some would camp along the creeks called Bordeaux, Dead Horse, and Crow Butte. The Sioux also camped in the area known as Mirage Flats located south of Hay Springs, Nebraska.

In the year 1923 or 1924, my parents decided to gather wild fruit in this area and we made camp there to gather fruit. Mother did not join in picking fruit and walked away from camp to be alone. We heard Mother singing and crying because the place where we had camped brought memories of her parents. Mother's father, Fast Thunder, had brought Chief Crazy Horse to this place and had then taken him to Fort Robinson. Chief Crazy Horse was later killed at Fort Robinson.

When my Grandfather, Fast Thunder, Indian Scout for the United States Army, died the Army gave Grandfather's flag to Grandmother and just before her death, Grandmother gave the flag to me. This same United States flag is now in my possession and the flag shall remain in my possession until my death.

My will states, that upon my death, if Mr. Edward Kadlecek, Hay Springs, Nebraska has prepared a Museum where the flag can be displayed, the flag shall remain in the Museum. If Mr. Kadlecek fails to prepare a Museum or should sell his property to another person, the flag shall be given to the nearest living relative of Fast Thunder. I am doing this because the place where Mr. Kadlecek now lives is the exact location where my Grandfather used to camp.

I am reaching old age and this information is needed to establish the location of the last stopping place of Chief Fast Thunder and Chief Crazy Horse. I hope that someday we will receive some kind of benefit because of those who lived in those days. What I have said here are the true facts as I know them.

MARY PACER
October 23, 1962

Indian Area

My name is George Red Bear, age 85, of Pine Ridge, South Dakota. My father's name is Red Bear, he was an Indian Scout for the United States Army. At that time, my father was traveling under the command of Bear Skin and White Hat. The Rosebud and Oglala Sioux were camped all along the valley from Beaver Creek, old Comer's place and up to Fort Robinson, Nebraska. At that time they heard that an Indian Scout went after Chief Crazy Horse. Upon arrival at Fort Robinson, Chief Crazy Horse was stabbed in the back which killed him. After the death of Chief Crazy Horse, the Sioux were moved to Thunder Butte. They camped there for about one year. From Thunder Butte, the Oglala Sioux moved back to this area and settled from Kyle, South Dakota to Oglala, South Dakota, now known as the Pine Ridge Indian Reservation. At that time my father, Red Bear, commanded two companies. These two companies camped at the place where White Clay Creek flows into the White River. Now that from what I personally know is that where Kadlecek is now residing is an Indian area.

GEORGE RED BEAR
November 5, 1962

Statement

I am 95 years old. I was born in 1871, right below or north of Chimney Rock near what is now Bayard, Nebraska. I was 6 years old when Crazy Horse was killed. When I was grown I was in the army. I was stationed at Fort Crook in Company I, 2nd Regiment. I was with Frank Goings. I am the only one surviving.

My father, Philip Red Bear, was a scout. I, Howard Red Bear, was a soldier. My son, Isaac Red Bear, was killed in World War II. My grandson, John Red Bear, has just returned and been discharged from the army. Four generations have served.

According to my father, he and Crazy Horse were close companions, in fact they were third degree cousins. Crazy Horse was a great fighter. He never used a gun. He used a tomahawk. He had the fastest horse and with his tomahawk that was all the weapons he used. This man Crazy Horse was not big—he was medium sized—with light hair and light complexion. An old man named High Eagle, now dead, resembled Crazy Horse's face and his build.

My father said that Crazy Horse was a great leader of war and this was known among other tribes. When opposing tribes knew he was the leader they retreated and didn't fight. They were afraid of Crazy Horse. White soldiers always tried to capture him all the time. So the soldiers talked to some of the chiefs to help capture Crazy Horse. They tried to get other chiefs to betray Crazy Horse. Which they finally did. Of course some refused to help these soldiers and they told Crazy Horse and he said, "They'll never capture me. As long as I live and am able to fight the white soldiers will never catch me."

As a troop was preparing to capture Crazy Horse with the help of the chiefs, one chief told Crazy Horse about it. He told Crazy Horse that the whites were trying to get Crazy Horse to quit fighting. But he said, "I'll never quit. I'll fight as long as I'm able to fight."

There was a certain chief named Little Big Man. He went to Crazy Horse and told him that they were trying to take him to prison, but if they did he, Little Big Man, would go with him. This Little Big Man was jealous of Crazy Horse and while pretending to be his friend wanted to get rid of him. Crazy Horse said to Little Big Man, "You and I will go north." Little Big Man agreed to go north, but was still trying to get rid of Crazy Horse.

They took off north. They met eight Indian riders. They thought these riders would go along. Instead the riders stopped Crazy Horse and Little Big Man. These riders (two of whom were Feather On Head and Lone Bull) persuaded Crazy Horse to go to the fort. They tricked Crazy Horse to come into the fort on business. So they really did not capture him. He trusted his companions and by their word he walked into his death trap. They know that this man or his companions who gave Crazy Horse away was promised something.

Later at the guard house he was stabbed from behind with a bayonet. According to my father Little Big Man held Crazy Horse when he was stabbed.

His father asked for the body and they granted him permission to bring it back to Beaver Valley where they had a wake on a certain tree. He departed from the wake on Beaver Creek with the body, but nobody knows where.

Crazy Horse had a close friend named Chips. They were camping together. Chips told that he was camping with the father of Crazy Horse, but the next morning when he got up the body was gone. He was the only one with Crazy Horse's father, but even he did not know what was done with it. At that time Chips couldn't see the travois tracks and they tried to find the tracks. Chips came clear to Porcupine and Pine Ridge, then back toward Fort Robinson, but never could find the tracks of the travois. When they had brought the body back to the Beaver Creek area, he promised he would tell Chips the next day where the body was buried. But if he did tell Chips, Chips never told it to anyone.

The father of Crazy Horse said the reason why he didn't want anyone to know the burial spot was he did not want any white or anyone of the jealous chiefs who had helped the white soldiers by betraying Crazy Horse to touch Crazy Horse's body. If anyone had touched his body there would have been another battle.

The people, relatives of Crazy Horse, said that the whites will never in the future get his body or anything that belongs to Crazy Horse.

At the time of Crazy Horse the Rosebuds and some Oglalas camped on Beaver. Nobody really claimed Beaver Creek, but the Rosebuds always camped there in the upper part of the camp with the Oglalas in the lower part or down stream. Near Beaver Creek there are some high hills where there was a fasting place. A lot of kinnikinnic which they liked to smoke grew along Beaver. Also the area was a safe place, a good hiding place with plenty of wood and food. On the high hills one could see many miles. My folks camped there on the Oglala side of the camp.

To make a fire we carried a piece of buffalo hide about a foot square. It was to hold some dry stuff and ashes. Holding a round piece of flint above, we would strike it so the sparks would fall on the dry material, then blow on it until it started to burn. When not in use it was tightly rolled to keep it very dry. We could start fires in this way in all weather even in a blizzard.

In making knives a certain bone in the back of the neck of a buffalo was used. They used a stone like one now used to whet knives to sharpen the blade. It took quite a while. A piece of green ash wood was used for the handle. It was split and pushed onto the blade. A tendon from the back of the leg of the buffalo was boiled then wrapped around the green ash wood to finish the handle. As the tendon dried it tightened and became very firm.

Before the whites came they used the shoulder blade for a hatchet or to dig. When the whites first came they gave the Indians small hatchets, but the Indians didn't know what to do with the hatchets. They tied them on a string of deerskin and wore them for necklaces.

I still have an old Indian spoon made from an animal horn.

The small straight pipe found on Beaver is very old. It was fashioned after the bone pipe. It was smoked the regular way, straight, like the Indian used to. After the whites came the style changed.

My father talked about a Sun Dance. However at the time of the Sun Dance four families went north hunting and my father was one of them, so missed out on the dance. There was a real old man, he died not long ago, his name was Left Heron. He told about that Sun Dance.

When I was at Beaver Creek on August 7, 1966, I placed two sticks crossing each other. The two sticks represent the Indian and the white who have learned to live together. Leave them and when I am gone it will remind you that I have been here.

HOWARD RED BEAR
August 13, 1966

A Historical Record

This is a historical record told by my grandmother, Charges At. She was the sixth daughter of Chief Red Cloud. She was born in

1862, and died on October 7, 1937, at the age of 75. Her husband, Kills Above, was born in 1865, and lived to be 81 years old.

Mrs. Charges At told me, Edgar Red Cloud, her grandson, about this Beaver Valley area where she had once lived. She told of places where they had once roamed. They had been so happy while they lived there. It was the chosen land of Crazy Horse and Fast Thunder. She told that there was a young man that was buried on a scaffold in a tree, but she didn't say who it was.

She also told about one of their last Sun Dances in the area. It was a sacred ground marked by rocks. This sacred ground was a place for a warrior to go to ask the medicine man for information concerning how to gain help to cure sickness, of his own or of his family, to find food, or to find an enemy to fight. The medicine man would be given a pipe as an offering. If he accepted, he smoked, then they went to the sacred ground to learn what was to be done. The warrior who wanted this help had to suffer to obtain it. He might be told to stand on a hill for four days, or in the creek, or sit cramped in a dugout. Maybe he would see a vision, or an animal might approach and tell him, "you have the power you ask." Then he went back to the medicine man, who interpreted what he had seen or heard and so declared his prayers had been answered.

From what Charges At said, the sacred ground was still here in this area.

The reason the Sioux picked this site for a camp was because it was in reach of timber, water, wild fruit, and wild game. In the fall of the year, the game was killed when it was fat. The meat was dried and stored in rawhide bags. The supply was preserved. Later in the fall they moved down to the Missouri River. They moved there in order to have an available supply of feed for their horses. They would cut the cottonwood trees and feed the bark to their horses. It kept the horses fat.

In the spring the Indians came back to the White River valleys. It was a place to hide in case of attack or invasion. In this area down along the creek bottom are solid butte clay banks. Higher on top there are walls. These banks and walls were used as carriers of

Edgar Red Cloud.

sound. In case someone was lost, or game was near, or an enemy coming, criers in the tribe would go to the wall and shout out towards the banks. The echo would bounce back and forth in the walled-in camp. The echo would carry throughout the whole camp. If the crier was on top of the buttes, his call could go for miles. The walls along the valley were called Beaver Walls, and the high point near the head of the wall was named Scout Hill. From there the Indians scouted for game, horses, enemies, and to observe weather conditions. It was possible to see a long way from the hill. There were trails leading into the valley from south, east, west, and north.

Near this area—west and a little north—was located Camp Sheridan, about an hour's walk down along Beaver Creek from Fast Thunder's camp. The Indians measured distance by the time it took to go that far. About one-fourth of a day of medium walking would be ten miles. A day of fast walking would be about fifty miles or possibly six miles an hour.

Not far from Fast Thunder's camp were Twin Buttes. This was a landmark for traveling as was Crow Butte farther to the west.

When this lady, Charges At, came into this area, she sang a song for Fast Thunder. The words of the song were:

My people, when you come into this area remember me,
Then Fast Thunder went away.

Her husband, Kills Above, said that his father's family had lived in this area, also.

EDGAR RED CLOUD
November 3, 1970

The Sun Dance

This ceremony is the only way the Indian worshipped before the white man came.

In mid-summer at the moon of ripe cherries, they would dance.

The sacred pole was a cottonwood tree. It must be a straight tree. About two-thirds of the way up there is a short branch, but the short one has no leaves. The one straight to the top has leaves. They have to find such a tree, sometimes they look all over for it. They use this tree because it is straight and has pretty leaves that shine and can be seen from long distances. They honor it because the Indian people use it for patterns for tipis and moccasins. The branch has a star in the center which represents the morning star. The bark is like grain with its vitamins.

The sacred pole represents the happy hunting ground. It is the Milky Way which lies across the sky. When an Indian dies, he is believed to travel the Milky Way. In the Milky Way, there is a short branch off the mainpart, about two-thirds across. Before an Indian dies, he has to have a red tatoo on his forehead, then when this person dies, his spirit travels this Milky Way to the divide. There is an old man or woman sitting there. When the spirit gets there, this man at the divide will notice him. If he has a red tatoo, he says to go straight on into the leaves and the leaves represent the happy hunting ground. Without the red tatoo he would fall back to earth.

This tree—before using or cutting—is offered to the Great Spirit with a peace pipe. The leaders choose a young Indian maid, about nine or ten years old. She chops once at the tree, then the helpers cut it down. The helpers bring it back to the sacred ground which is where the dance is to be held. On that special branch they tie wild fruit branches—Juneberry, cherry, and plum. They tie these in a bunch and put them into the tree crotch. They, also, cut out a small man and a buffalo from buffalo hide, and tie them in the leaves. Then the helpers stand up the tree like a post. Before packing the ground, they offer tobacco and flesh at the foot of the tree, then pack it.

A man who has promised the Great Spirit to sacrifice for healing of the sick or to forestall famine would make such an offering. This dancer who sacrifices himself must not eat or drink for four days. At night he rests under the pole. The dancer has his chest pierced with a three-corner shaped stick about the size of the little finger. This stick is a certain kind, mesquite, which never floats and won't burn. The dancer takes medicine from the medicine man, the director of the Sun Dance, so there is no need for a rest room. Food and water are carried in front of the dancer to make him suffer. The dancer has to dance with music and tom-toms. The singers are in groups of two or three and each day they change off. Special songs are used—Sun Dance songs—with the words of the songs made to make the dancers worry. The rib from the buffalo was made like a saw. It was used to cut the flesh if it didn't break from pulling.

The dancer, as well as the people, honor the colors that the Great Spirit gives them. There are six colors. First is the yellow—it represents the sun. The blue represents the blue sky; the green—mother earth; red—the red race; white—peace and purity; black—the night.

The dancer when pierced prays to the Great Spirit in the four directions of the wind. The prayers that the dancer says are: We pray to the Great Spirit where all things come; to the north, you have made the beautiful snow, the wild game, buffalos and beautiful pine trees, evergreen year-around, and northern lights; to the east, the day, sunlight, knowledge, religion; to the south, the beautiful rivers and creeks, wild fruit, pretty flowers; to the west, the sunset where all human beings are at rest, and bring us to another day. We know the Great Spirit is everywhere. That is why we pray to the four winds.

Before this dance started, the dancer went to take a sweat bath. The hut is made of twelve willows. In this bath there are rocks heated. They take rocks to the alter in the center of the hut. In presenting rocks to the altar a forked stick is used to handle the hot rocks. They pour water on the rocks to make this steam. This steam purifies his body.

EDGAR RED CLOUD
November 3, 1970

Fast Thunder's Life

Fast Thunder was a right hand band-chief of warrior supreme Chief Crazy Horse. He was a noted and well-known first Sioux Indian enlisted in the United States Army. The Government of the

United States had chosen a tract of land near Crawford, Nebraska for the Sioux Tribe to settle as an Indian Reservation. At the time some of the Sioux lived at the place of Beaver Creek, which place is now a residence of Edward F. Kadlecek, ten miles north of Hay Springs, Nebraska.

Chief Crazy Horse voluntarily moved in from the north plains to the said place at the Beaver Creek to live with his Sioux Tribe. Chief Crazy Horse had a conversation with Fast Thunder, in which he stated he had no desire to make war and that he wanted to live in peace and he agreed to appear at the United States Army Post—Fort Robinson, to meet the Army Commander. When Chief Crazy Horse started for the said Army Post, he was escorted by Fast Thunder and several other friends. As Chief Crazy Horse arrived at the fort and walked toward the commander's office he noticed the guard was on duty—walking back and forth. One of the other Sioux informed him with false ideas—that he will be locked up in the guardhouse, if he ever gets into the commander's office. As he heard this language, he turned around and started away from the fort. As he started off, then, from right behind the cold steel of a soldier's bayonet speared into his ribs by an Indian Scout of the United States Army—Little Big Man. The parents of Chief Crazy Horse arrived at the place shortly after he was killed and they picked the body up and loaded it on the travois. They hauled it to the place of the Sioux Camp at the Beaver Creek. From there, there is no signs of where the body was buried. The parents kept Chief Crazy Horse's body secret to avoid the purloin of the body by the white people and the United States Army.

Before this, Fast Thunder had gone to Fort Robinson to canvass the location chosen by the United States Government for the Sioux Tribe as Indian Reservation. Fast Thunder found that the location was not suitable for an Indian Reservation. Then he went and chopped the United States flag pole down, which flag was erected by the United States Government to dedicate the Indian Reservation of the Oglala Sioux Tribe. He brought and erected the said flag at the place of Pine Ridge, S. D., now Indian Reservation of the Oglala

Sioux Tribe. Several months later Fast Thunder went out to the north plains to bring part of Crazy Horse's band to the Indian Reservation, those who still dwelled in the badlands. One member of this band shot at Fast Thunder with a rifle, because he accused Fast Thunder of forcing this band to the Indian Reservation to take the ward-ship under the United States Military Department. They thought there would be great hardship under the said department. Fast Thunder continually upheld his peace and maintained his control over this band until he brought them into the Reservation. The members of this band thought it would be a great change from the life on their happy hunting ground to the hardship of being wards of the government.

Several years later, Fast Thunder chose a piece of land three and one-half miles north of Wounded Knee, South Dakota, and lived there for the rest of his life. He farmed many acres of land and raised good crops of small grains. He was the first Indian to own a horse powered threshing machine—to harvest his small grain every year. He also raised large numbers of livestock. On the first round-up, he had seven hundred and seven head of horses and seven hundred and seven head of cattle. For the reason that he raised the identical number of seven hundred and seven head of horses to the number of seven hundred and seven head of cattle in the same year, the Stock Detective selected the mark of 707 for Fast Thunder to brand his horses and cattle.

Fast Thunder was the first Indian to employ white people to take care of his residence. One of the white men employees started his own farm and ranch with his earnings of the payment of horses and cattle paid to him by Fast Thunder, after said employee tendered his resignation from the employment of Fast Thunder's residence.

The Fast Thunder owned peace pipe with procupine quilled stem is now in the possession of Paul Red Star of Wounded Knee, South Dakota.

PAUL RED STAR
February 7, 1964

Statement

Alfred Ribman, 87 years of age, a member of the Oglala Sioux Tribe, states that Crazy Horse was a famous and unexcelled warrior. It was believed that divine influence guided his soul, mind, and physical being. The great warrior met sudden death in the year of 1877. The last observation of the original and genuine Sun Dance Ceremony was solemnized by the Sioux at the foot of the Beaver Mountain located on the south part of the chosen land where the Sioux camped on Beaver Creek. The ceremony was observed on behalf of Crazy Horse. There were five warriors making the supreme sacrifice for their great leader. The five warriors were Eagle Thunder, Black Fox, and three Kicking Bear brothers. Fast Thunder was ordained a ceremonial chief by the spiritual incision overseer who penetrated the flesh of the five warriors, because Fast Thunder had been pierced in several previous ceremonies.

There are five large rocks set in the area of the Sun Dance which represented the five warriors who offered the extreme sacrifice, and the one large rock set on the west of five large rocks was the ceremonial altar where the offerings were placed during the observation of the ceremony. The five warriors who were cousins of Crazy Horse were braves and vigorous battle men of distinction.

The great Kicking Bear—father of the three Kicking Bear brothers—had been shot on his forehead with a steel spear-point arrow at the battle. The steel spear remained penetrated in his forehead after the arrow had been taken off from his forehead. He lived with a steel spear on his forehead for years. One of his cousins pulled the steel spear out of his head after he died.

The bodies of the great Kicking Bear and Short Bull were given a tree burial in the sepulcher tree. This sepulcher tree used for warrior burial is very large, and of many hundreds of years old. It still stands in the chosen land where the Sioux camped on the Beaver Creek. A body of another warrior was buried on another sepulcher tree; that tree, too, still stands in the same area.

Warrior Chief Crazy Horse requested the warrior cousins that, at his death his body be painted with red war paint and plunged into the fresh water (it did not matter where) to be restored back to life, otherwise his bones would be turned into stone and his joints into flint in his grave, but his spirit would rise. But the warriors were in such a condition of extreme mourning at that time when he was killed, that no one remembered his request.

Warrior Chief Crazy Horse and his band of warriors protected and defended the Sioux Tribe with great force against the enemies and won many battles.

Warrior Chief Crazy Horse rode his war pony up to the top of the Beaver Mountain and consummated his final fast in a solemn promise to end his war trail, just two days before he was killed on September 5, 1877. After Warrior Chief Crazy Horse was killed, the Oglala Sioux and the Rosebud Sioux Tribes separated.

ALFRED RIBMAN
February 24, 1966

Early History

My grandfather camped on Beaver Creek before I was born. He told things to my young uncle, Plenty Bird, who asked him silly questions. How did you get along without [government] issue [of food and clothing]? We used buffalo hide in winter. How did they skin buffalos? We used buffalo ribs for knives to skin the buffalo.

Plenty Bird asked Grandma how she tanned skins. She soaked the skin in water, then scraped and stretched it and rubbed it. In the hills they found sharp rocks to tan the hide and use to make dresses. Deer hides were used for dresses. Buffalo hides were used for covers, and blankets. Skin on legs was used for sleeves, as they had no scissors. She didn't cut the skin to make a dress. Needles—some kind of thorn, also sharp bones, were used to make holes then sew with sinew. She made mittens and shirts of hide. Now they soak skin in neatsfoot oil for three days, then soak in water, then work over a scythe with the dull side fastened along a tree, until it is soft.

How did you sleep? We slept in buffalo hides to keep us warm. The buffalo had hair. We turned it inside to keep warm. We could even crawl under snow and stay warm. In winter we made a shelter. The men went to hunt and the women dug the ground for a fire place. We gathered sage for mattresses and covered it with hide. The tent was made of hides. The top of the tipi was open for a chimney. They set poles with sharp points to hold flaps to draw the smoke out.

How did they chop wood? The women went out to gather wood. They had to camp close to wood. The women used their feet to break wood. They gathered dry wood, because it would break easily.

What kind of bread did you have? None. They ate meat.

What did you drink? Water and soup.

How did you cook without pots? We had to hunt and kill deer, then barbecue them. At that time, they didn't have bad teeth. They ate kidney and liver raw. We killed the buffalo, cleaned the guts. The four corners on the paunch were fastened on long stakes. The

Stella Swift Bird.

meat was cut in long strips. It was cooked with hot rocks in the paunch. They ate the paunch, too.

How did you make fire? They kept dry inner cottonwood bark in a bag. To start a fire they struck together two flint rocks to make sparks. When the sparks landed on the dry bark, they burned. Special rocks were used to cook. Rock that wouldn't crack when heated and wet with cold water. When Grandfather went toward Chadron, he always took rocks home cause rocks at Wounded Knee would crack. They used no salt. Sometimes they got salt at Salt Lake. The bladder was used for a water bag. The bladder could be dried and used again. They rubbed it to soften it while it was a bit damp. A knife was made from buffalo ribs. Bark was used for dishes.

How did you make saddles? The hip bones of the buffalo were used for saddles. The socket hole was used to fasten on stirrups.

Quills were colored with red and yellow clay. Grandmother dug it. She baked it in balls of mud over certain wood fire for heat. After it was baked they put it into water and boiled quills in it. Blue was made from some kind of root.

My grandfather, Fast Thunder had scars on his back and chest. He said, "I danced, the sticks were pierced into the flesh and I drug the buffalo heads. I had only one sister. I hunted and never stayed near my folks. I went to other tribes to steal their best horses. When I went back my sister was dying in bed. I wanted my sister to get well. In the middle of the summer, I prayed to the Great Spirit and danced. When she got well I had to dance."

Sun Dance poles were used on reservations. My grandfather told that he danced there on Beaver Creek. On one of those hills at Beaver he stood, not sat. Four days and four nights he stood, so she, his sister, would get well. He prayed and got an answer. A snake came and talked to him. It was a spirit. Even little birds came and talked to him. He fasted for his mother at Scottsbluff. He fasted for his father, brother, aunt, uncle, cousin. That's how much he loved them. One fast was in Montana, one in the Black Hills, one in North Dakota, and one on top of Bear Butte, always on the highest butte he could find.

When people came to the Sun Dance each added a skin to the shade. When the dance was held, all children stayed in the tent. Dogs were tied up. Everyone was quiet and all prayed. When a man came from the hill after a fast, he came to the sweat bath. They listened as he told what he had seen and heard. The next morning before the sun was up, he started dancing. All day he looked right at the sun. The old ones all sat with heads down and cried and prayed as the men danced. While looking at the sun, they saw signs or answers for prayers.

My grandfather was afraid of water. He dreamed about bears. He stayed out in open prairies. After a raid, three of them, he and two friends, went to a coyote den. One was guard, the rest hid in the sage. Grandfather looked back on their trail. He saw a buffalo trailing them. They ran to the guard. The only place for protection was the coyote den. They crawled in. The buffalo bumped the rock, his breath smelled funny. Then in the night the coyote talked to Fast Thunder in his sleep. It was time for her to go out. She howled after she got out. Grandfather said it was clear. Grandfather dreamed again. The coyote said to go to the creek and kill meat. Something will protect Grandfather. They crawled out and came to the creek and killed a deer. They ate liver and left the rest for the coyote. They walked all day along the creek as the coyote had told them to do. At evening they rested, they made a shelter of cottonwood bark. Grandfather sat by the entry. They all slept except Grandfather. When he heard something, his heart started jumping. A bear said, "Follow me." Grandfather woke the others and they followed the bear. The bear led them, as he was a holy bear. At other times the bear had told him where to dig roots for sick people. Since bears are afraid of water, he was afraid of water. The bear led them back to Beaver Creek where his folks were camped. They had moved so much Fast Thunder didn't know where they were living.

He Dog was a chief, he also came from Beaver.

Fast Thunder was a traveler. He and another man were coming back from the hills on the other side of Hot Springs. A buffalo was chasing them. There was no place to hide, for they were in a little draw with a few pines. Grandfather prayed for his holy bear. As grandfather was leading, a short, little man with long hair came. He led them to a cave—a spirit hole—then he said, "Just squeeze in, but don't come any farther." They could feel the wind draw and blow. The little man disappeared. At that time they called it spirit hole, but now it is Wind Cave. When they went in Grandfather's heart was jumpy and the other man was crying.

"Don't be scared, pray," Grandfather said. Grandfather took his bow to feel around, but it was a drop-off. The buffalo stuck in his head, but couldn't come in. All afternoon and all night they stayed as they were afraid to go out. But the buffalo had gone.

Hot Springs was called holy water or holy place. When people got sick they went there to drink the holy water. They drank four times and each time it had a different taste. They drank four mouthfuls and prayed.

Fast Thunder went around with Crazy Horse. Crazy Horse dreamed about things that were going to happen. Crazy Horse didn't care to get married. A woman went to him to get married, but he just went off alone, so he wasn't married. Crazy Horse's father and his family took sick and all were dead so there were no relations. His mother had sisters.

Sometimes Fast Thunder met Crazy Horse out and they hunted together. Crazy Horse dreamed about the future, so he always knew ahead what was going to happen and how to plan. He was a smart man. He was a brave man afraid of nothing.

Fast Thunder and Pourier worked together. Pourier went east and Fast Thunder gave him his best horse. When Pourier came back he brought two wagons with oxen and yokes. With the oxen they plowed. He brought chickens and ducks and oats. They were the first Indians to plant oats.

One time Fast Thunder and a friend went to a camp of Crow Indians and took their best horses. Presently they were surrounded, but Fast Thunder said, "We'll get away."

He chewed some kind of weed and covered the horses and both men. They left rawhide blankets over the bushes. They rode so fast down the valley that they really didn't know how. Later from the top of a nearby hill they watched the Crows kill the "rawhides."

STELLA SWIFT BIRD
May 5, 1969

Statement

I am Frank White Buffalo Man from Little Eagle, South Dakota. I am a Hunkpapa Sioux. I am the only close descendent of Sitting Bull. My father was Sitting Bull's son. I am sixty-six years old.

I went to school at the Salem Indian School in Chemawa, Oregon, and at the Black Hills Teacher's College in Spearfish, South Dakota. I am a student of Indian lore and am interested in Indian tradition.

I believe the Indian Spirit is a sleeping giant and that it is coming back to life. The last time the Great Spirit came back was in 1859. In four or five generations the end will come to pass and the Great Spirit will come to life. When the Buffalo Woman brought the pipe, the buffalo was standing up—now it is lying down. I am the only one on the Standing Rock Reservation who uses the pipe to pray and does the Peace Pipe Ceremony. The Spotted Eagle is the Sacred Bird and only its feathers are used on the pipe.

The Indians have a Red Power which is a Spiritual Power. I believe the old medicine man had power and that their spirits are still living and that Crazy Horse's Spirit is still around and that perhaps I could talk to his Spirit, for this is the Continent of the Great Spirit.

Sitting Bull was the Chief of all the Sioux. Crazy Horse was second in command as War Chief. My aunt, whose father was a sub-chief, was a Hunkpapa Sioux. She knew who Crazy Horse was. She said Crazy Horse was about five feet, seven inches tall. He had kind of lighter hair. On Cheyenne River there was someone who looked like Crazy Horse. Crazy Horse had a scar. Crazy Horse humbled himself. As popular as he was, he never mixed with the crowd. He dreamed of red hawks and received power. Because of his power he had two or three red hawk feathers that hung down, fastened to the back of his hair. He never tried to dress well like other chiefs. He was always by himself. He made his own power. When someone wanted him, they could always get his wife, Black Shawl, to go after him. He dreamed about ants. He grabbed ant hill dirt and threw it to the four winds for protection in battle. When he went into battle he wanted to accomplish something. In a battle with the Crows he killed many warriors. Afterwards his people tried to help him from his horse. As they did he turned to stone, but as his feet touched the earth he came back to life.

I believe we are sacred people and everything was done in a sacred way—like in the Sun Dance, the sacred tree has to be a cottonwood tree, for it has the star inside.

When the tribe had their meetings, they had technical thinkers who had charity in their hearts. These sat in the chief's lodge. No one else could put a foot inside. Each of these men carried a stick. If any one of these chief members committed something wrong, the others would spit on his stick and throw it out, then he couldn't come back to the council.

My people are now confused. They should be taught the Indian Lore. They should be taught to respect the Sacred Red Hoop.

All of Sitting Bull's descendents took part in a Sun Dance at Little Eagle to pray for rain and it rained. This was about thirty years ago.

Long time ago the people taught children by giving advice and talking nice to them. They played games with a whip and a bone, on the ice. It prompted accuracy. They had many good athletes.

The interpreters in the old days often made mistakes and were wrong because they did not have an education and did not know how to interpret correctly. Big Leggings and Brewer were interpreters for Sitting Bull.

There were two groups of people at Standing Rock Agency. The people at Fort Yates were Eastern Dakotas and were Yanktonais. Two Bear was their leader. They were peace loving people. The Hunkpapa Sioux from Little Eagle, Bull Head, and Wakpala were the ones who fought against Custer.

Long ago some people, government officials, wanted to meet with

Frank White Buffalo Man.

Sitting Bull. He was out hunting. Gall, Crow King, and Grass were chiefs, but the officials would not talk to them, so the Indians brought Sitting Bull. Sitting Bull picked up a handful of dirt and said he couldn't give them this much.

Near Little Eagle and in the surrounding areas are some interesting landmarks which were named by the Indians long ago. This is how Black Horse Butte west of McIntosh received its name. A Black Horse with a long tail came to the top of the butte in a sacred way. It stood on top then turned to face each of the four directions. The people tried to catch it by surrounding the butte, but the horse was gone. Black brings bad luck, and the following summer a cyclone came and destroyed the homes. Takes Blanket was drawn up into the wind where he lost his clothes. Coming down he grabbed a plum bush and saved himself, so he was one who lived through a wind funnel.

On a butte past Rattlesnake Butte, the people made designs of deer and other markings. The Medicine men went there to gain power.

Elk Horn Butte received its name because elks went there to shed their horns.

FRANK WHITE BUFFALO MAN
May 12, 1969

Finding of the Peace Pipe

A peace pipe was found along Capa Wakpa (Beaver Creek) by Everette White Dress, age 28, Pine Ridge, So. Dak. The peace pipe was found on the spot of land where the Earthen dam, known as the Edward Kadlecek reservoir, ties into the west bank of Beaver Creek, this is the area where Fast Thunder had camped and also the area of the last stop of Chief Crazy Horse. In the month of April, 1957, Everette White Dress started working for Mr. Kadlecek, clearing timber from the side and along Beaver Creek within the area of Mr. Kadlecek's residence. On or about the first week of May, 1957, a peace pipe was found lying with the wooden part gone to rot.

It was learned that Fort Sheridan was stationed on a place four or five miles northwest of Mr. Kadlecek's residence and where the Indians camped along the Beaver Creek. The place mentioned and the residence of Mr. Kadlecek is located ten miles northwest of Hay Springs, Nebraska and may be reached on the Beaver Creek road that ties into Hiway No. 20 at Hay Springs, Nebraska.

EVERETTE WHITE DRESS
October 29, 1962.

Statement

I, Joe White Face, was born July 28, 1903 at Porcupine, Shannon County, South Dakota. I have made my home on the place where I was born.

I had talks with some of the older Indians, who are still living, concerning Chief Crazy Horse and Beaver Creek. I have been told that Crazy Horse was a great leader and fighter and he was a leader of the Sioux Tribe. These men who made the statements are descendents of Crazy Horse's followers and they have given their statement according to what they were told by their fathers and grandfathers who were companions of Crazy Horse. These statements are nothing but the truth as in early days when an Indian brought news to report to the village he was sworn in by taking a puff on the peace pipe and swore under four items: a hole in the ground, a gun shell, an arrow, and a knife. If he lied one of these would kill him.

Now Crazy Horse was not arrested. By a jealous Indian the white soldiers lured him into Fort Robinson to be taken into custody. As he was taken toward the guard house and noticed bars on the door, one Indian shouted at him to do something, which he attempted to do. But a white soldier stabbed him in the kidney with a bayonet. He fell over and died.

When his father heard about it he went and requested that he be granted the permission to take the body; his request was granted. He took the body to Beaver Creek where Oglala and Rosebud Sioux

Joe White Face.

were camping. He placed the body on a certain tree, which is still living, and all the people went to where he lay in state to honor him. Early next morning his body was removed and his father took the body alone as he did not want the white soldiers to do any more harm and he did not trust anyone. So he took the body some place in the Beaver Creek area where they believe he was buried, because traveling was slow and usually the September month gets real warm. So Crazy Horse's father cannot go very far with the body.

I was told that Red Cloud was the Chief of the Oglala Sioux Tribe and he had four other chiefs under him namely, Chief Little Wound, Chief American Horse, Chief No Water, and Chief Turning Hawk. These chiefs were well known by other tribes of Indians. Chief Spotted Tail was the Chief of the Rosebud.

So these men: Thomas American Horse, age 96, Thomas White

Face, age 94, and Howard Red Bear, age 95, affirm that Crazy Horse was buried some place in the Beaver Creek area.

To the best of my knowledge this is a true statement.

JOE WHITE FACE
September 6, 1966

Statement

My name is Standing Bull. Now at the present time I am known as Thomas White Face and am 94 years of age. My family name is Standing Bull. When baptized I was given my father's name of White Face. The church gave me the first name of Thomas. When enrolled in the census, I was given my father's name of White Face instead of Standing Bull. I was one of the first councilmen in Frank Wilson's administration, when it was first organized. My son, Joe White Face, was also a councilman, and Tribal Judge for six years for the Porcupine and Kyle District. My grandson, Isaac White Face, is at present a councilman.

My father and mother knew Crazy Horse well. Crazy Horse was small in stature, but a brave man and a leader.

The white people and soldiers tried to take him as a prisoner so they could control his following, which was great. The day he came in to Fort Robinson, his cousin Thunder Hawk was with him. As they approached the log house his cousin noticed that it was the guard house. He saw bars on the windows and an iron door. His cousin told him that he must do something. Crazy Horse resisted and was stabbed from behind with a bayonet through the kidney. He was bleeding very bad and dying shortly after he was stabbed. Thunder Hawk with the help of others picked the body up and got a spring wagon pulled by a team of mules from the fort. They put the body on the spring wagon and hauled it a short distance from the fort and there awaited the arrival of his father whom they had notified. His father arrived not very long afterwards. He asked the soldiers that he be granted permission to take the body. He did not want to be bothered by any white people or anyone else. He wanted the body left to him and some of his friends. The request was granted and they took the body, placed it on a travois, and headed east for Beaver Creek, which was a well known creek and camping ground of the Oglalas and Brulés.

Here the body was prepared for burial. It was temporarily placed in a burial tree, which was an elm tree. It is still a live tree today showing that it was a burial tree. It was in this elm tree for a night and a day, where the wake was held. A multitude of people came to honor him at the wake, singing war songs and sad songs. A feast was held at midnight and the next day at noon. That night the father of Crazy Horse took the body from the tree and buried it in the vicinity of what some call Marker Hills, Twin Hills, or Beaver Mountain. Traveling was slow in those days and he did not go very far with the body. No one to this day knows the exact location of his grave, but his father came back early next morning, bleeding from arms and legs, singing sad songs, and hair cut off.

When all the people left the camp for the Missouri, he did not have the body. Descendants of the followers of Crazy Horse who had lived at Fort Yates on the Standing Rock Reservation in North Dakota have verified that his father did not have the body when they left the Beaver Creek camp, namely Standing Elk, Running Bear, and Fat Crane. The first two came back, and Standing Elk died at Porcupine and Running Bear died at Allen. A lot of others beside these two have verified the same thing.

When the Sioux were camped on the Little Big Horn, the Rosebuds, Oglalas, Cheyennes, and two others were camped on the north side. Only part of the village showed. One morning some of the women went out wild turnip digging. Around noon the women came home on the run leaving their digging tools out there when they sighted the cavalry approaching the camp. They reported the same to the village headquarters. Leaders called all the warriors together and prepared for a battle. All got ready and gathered on a hill northeast of the village and waited for Crazy Horse to arrive, which he finally did. They started an attack, so the cavalry dismounted and started firing. Crazy Horse did not stop, so they

Thomas White Face (standing) and family.

mounted their horses, but the warriors surrounded them. Crazy
Horse used a club instead of gun or bow and arrow. This happened
around noon. All of the troops were wiped out in a short time.
Because Crazy Horse killed all of the soldiers the other troops were
really mad at him, for they knew he was the leader.

The soldiers did everything they could to capture him and
Wounded Knee Massacre was a revenge. Custer's Battle was a fair
fight, but the Wounded Knee was not.

Beaver Creek Sun Dance. Kicking Bear and brothers, and Walking Eagle with three or four others were the main dancers according
to my father and mother. I was there with them at the dance.
Turning Eagle and Standing Bull (my father) with a few others were
the main dancers in 1882 south of Mission Town, close to Spring
Creek. The same year as the dance held on White Clay Creek.

THOMAS WHITE FACE (*thumbprint*)
August 10, 1966

Jerome Wolf Ears.

Talk of Jerome Wolf Ears

I am now at the age of 80, Post Office, Pine Ridge, South Dakota. From older people, say while the Sioux's were camping along Beaver Creek many years ago before the Sioux's made their settlement here on the Pine Ridge Reservation, Chief Crazy Horse visited the camp there, somewhere's east of Chadron, Nebraska. From there, he went to Fort Robinson where he was killed from what I heard, his body was brought back to this camp along Beaver Creek. This place must be the place where the Sioux's used to camp because of finding of the peace pipe at Mr. Edward F. Kadlecek's place by Mr. Everette White Dress.

JEROME WOLF EARS
November 14, 1963

Interview with Cleveland Black Crow

Indian people still return to Beaver Valley to take part in a Vision Quest. Frank Kicking Bear in his statement said that in 1942, Amos

Black Crow, provided additional information about the fast. He said:

It was in the middle of June when the seven people made their trip from Wounded Knee, South Dakota. There were Amos Black Crow and his wife, Ada; son, Cleveland; Amos's parents, Mr. and Mrs. Austin Black Crow; and relatives, Mr. James Eagle Bear and his wife, Stella. They journeyed to Beaver Valley with two teams, wagons and tents. On arrival they turned their hobbled horses loose to graze, then they set up their camps on a little flat of higher ground where the wind didn't swirl around as much as it did in the canyon.

At first Amos planned to fast on Scout Point, but after checking on it, he decided to go to Beaver Mountain. Amos fasted there four days and four nights. The first two days he prayed for the boys in World War II and for peace among nations to aid all people of the earth. The second two days he spent in appealing to the Great Spirit for guidance, as his main purpose in fasting was to gain help for his people. He prayed that the Indian generations would increase and live a better life. He asked that his people be cared for. On the fifth day, Cleveland and the Grandmother went to the top of Beaver Mountain to pray with Amos. That evening they brought him back to camp. On the sixth day they returned to their homes at Wounded Knee.

When Cleveland revisited Beaver Valley in 1968, he said that coming back brought sad memories of his parents and grandparents as all are now dead and only he and two sisters are left. At the Sun Dance Grounds, Cleveland commented that his grandparents had compared the shelf-like clearing back of and above the grounds to a balcony just full of people and horses when the Sun Dance for Crazy Horse was held.

Cleveland Black Crow said that right after Crazy Horse was killed at Fort Robinson, the image of a rider on a white horse appeared in the clouds.

February 29, 1968

THOMAS AMERICAN HORSE (1869-1963) was the eldest son of Chief American Horse and was a young boy when Crazy Horse was killed.

JOSEPH BLACK ELK (1895-1977) was the nephew of Chief Black Elk and a half-brother of Peter Bordeaux.

JOHN BLACK SMITH (1879-1969) was a rancher on White Clay Creek.

PETER BORDEAUX (1877-?) was the nephew of Louis Bordeaux, the interpreter between the Lakota and the army at Spotted Tail Agency.

JAMES CHASE IN MORNING (1888-?) heard stories about Crazy Horse from his father who was a young man when the chief was killed.

HENRY CROW DOG (1898-   ) is a well-known medicine man and Lakota historian. His father lived on Beaver Creek.

JESSIE (MEANS) ROMERO EAGLE HEART (1905-1972) was a granddaughter of Fast Thunder.

CHARLES FIRE THUNDER (1890-1974) was the son of Fire Thunder, a friend of Crazy Horse.

AUSTIN GOOD VOICE FLUTE (1885-1966) was a minister of the Episcopal church.

LAWSON R. GREGG (1912-   ) is part Osage and grew up at Edgemont, South Dakota.

DORA HIGH WHITE MAN (1883-1964) was a survivor of the Wounded Knee Massacre of 1890.

JULIA HOLLOW HORN BEAR (?-?) was the granddaughter of Battiste Good and the niece of White Woman One Butte who cleaned the body of Crazy Horse in preparation for burial.

CARL IRON SHELL (?-?) was a descendant of Chief Iron Shell, the cousin of Chief Crow Dog.

FRANK KICKING BEAR (1889-1965) was the son of Kicking Bear, a close friend of Crazy Horse.

MATHEW H. KING (1903-   ) is a grandson of Fast Thunder.

MARY (MEANS) PACER (1893-1974) was a granddaughter of Fast Thunder and a sister of Jessie Romero Eagle Heart.

GEORGE RED BEAR (1877-1964) was a medicine man.

HOWARD RED BEAR (1871-1968) was a small boy when Crazy Horse was killed. His father was a third cousin of the war chief.

EDGAR RED CLOUD (1896-1977) was the great-grandson of Chief Red Cloud.

PAUL RED STAR (1895-   ) is the eldest grandson of Fast Thunder.

ALFRED RIBMAN (1878-1969) was a cowboy and was well-versed in Lakota history.

STELLA SWIFT BIRD (1896-   ) is the sister of Paul Red Star and granddaughter of Fast Thunder.

FRANK WHITE BUFFALO MAN (1903-   ) is a grandson of Sitting Bull.

EVERETTE WHITE DRESS (1931-1980) found the little red pipe.

JOSEPH WHITE FACE (1904-1975) was a councilman and tribal judge, proficient in translating Lakota into English.

THOMAS WHITE FACE (1872-1967) was the son of Standing Bull, a medicine man, who knew Crazy Horse.

JEROME WOLF EARS (1884-1963) lived west of Pine Ridge with Red Cloud's people.

NOTES

Abbreviations
NSHS Nebraska State Historical Society
CIA Commissioner of Indian Affairs

Chapter 1

1. David Humphries Miller, *Ghost Dance* (New York· Duell, Sloan and Pearce, 1959), p. 286.
2. Eli S. Ricker, Garnett Interview, NSHS, MS 8, Roll 2, Tablet 9-17.
3. Ibid., Roll 1, p. 10.

Chapter 2

1. George E. Hyde, *Spotted Tail's Folk: A History of the Brulé Sioux* (Norman: University of Oklahoma Press, 1961), p. 5.
2. Garrick Mallery, "Picture Writing of the American Indian," in *Tenth Annual Report of the Bureau of Ethnology* (Washington, D.C.: GPO, 1893), p. 290.

Chapter 3

1. J.G. Hamilton to CIA, 1876, Spotted Tail Agency, NSHS, MS 2723, Roll 841.
2. John H. King, Orders, September 8, 1874, Camp Sheridan Letters, Box 1, NSHS, RG 2494.
3. Anson Mills, *My Story* (Washington, D.C.: Press of Byron S. Adams, 1919), p. 393.
4. E.A. Howard to CIA, September 14, 1874, Whetstone Agency, NSHS, MS 2723, Roll 927.
5. Howard to Major E.F. Townsend, January 10, 1875, Camp Sheridan, NSHS, MS 2723, Roll 840.
6. Spotted Tail Agency to Post Adjutant, Camp Sheridan, August 15, 1876, NSHS, MS 2723, Roll 841.
7. Cleveland to CIA, Spotted Tail Agency, NSHS, MS 2723, Roll 841.
8. George Hyde, *Spotted Tail's Folk: A History of the Brulé Sioux* (Norman: University of Oklahoma Press, 1961), p. 230.
9. Letters Received, Office of Indian Affairs, Spotted Tail Agency, NSHS, MS 2723, Roll 841.

Chapter 4

1. Eli S. Ricker, NSHS, MS 8, Roll 1, p. 72.
2. Ibid., p. 75.
3. George Hyde, *Spotted Tail's Folk: A History of the Brulé Sioux* (Norman: University of Oklahoma Press, 1961), p. 250.
4. Doane A. Robinson, *A Brief History of South Dakota* (New York: American Book Company, 1935), p. 15.

Chapter 5

1. E.P. Wilson, "The Story of the Oglala and the Brulé Sioux in the Pine Ridge Country of Northwest Nebraska in the Middle Seventies," *Nebraska History Magazine* 22 (January-March 1941): 19-21.
2. Frederick Means to Adjutant General at Omaha, August 11, 1876, Spotted Tail Agency, NSHS, MS 2723, Roll 841.
3. Irwin to CIA, July 8, 1877, NSHS, MS 2723, Roll 721.
5. George Manypenny to CIA, July 1877, NSHS, MS 2723, Roll 841.
6. Benjamin Shapp to CIA, August 15, 1877, NSHS, MS 2723, Roll 721.
7. Ibid.
8. Eli S. Ricker, NSHS, MS 8, Roll Tablet 2, p. 49.
9. Ibid., pp. 103-5.
10. Ibid., p. 105.
11. Shapp, *loc. cit.*
12. Ricker, Bordeaux Interview, NSHS, MS 8, Book 11, p. 72. Mari Sandoz, *Crazy Horse: The Strange Man of the Oglalas* (Lincoln: University of Nebraska Press, 1942), p. 378. E.A. Brininstool, "How Chief Crazy Horse Died," *Nebraska History* 2 (January 1929): 21.
13. Irwin to CIA, September 1, 1877, NSHS, MS 2723, Roll 721.
14. Ibid., August 31, 1877.
15. John G. Bourke, *On the Border with Crook* (New York: Charles Scribner's Sons, 1891), p. 120.
16. Letters Received, Office of Indian Affairs, Spotted Tail Agency, 1877, U.S. War Department Records, RG 2702, Box 1.

Chapter 6

1. Ricker, Bordeaux Interview, NSHS, MS 8, Roll 2, Tablets 9-17.
2. Red Cloud Agency to CIA, September 5, 1877, NSHS, MS 2723, Roll 721.
3. James Henry Cook, *Fifty Years on the Old Frontier* (New Haven: Yale University Press, 1923), p. 189.
4. E.A. Brininstool, "How Chief Crazy Horse Died," *Nebraska History* 12 (January 1929), p. 30.
5. Eli S. Ricker, NSHS, MS 8, Roll 1, Tablet 2, pp. 94-5.
6. Ibid.
7. Brininstool, *op. cit.*, pp. 27-9. David Humphries Miller, *Ghost Dance* (New York: Duell, Sloan and Pearce, 1959), p. 287. Mari Sandoz, *Hostiles and Friendlies* (Lincoln: University of Nebraska Press, 1959), p. 110.

8. Brininstool, *op. cit.*, p. 29.

9. Ricker, *loc. cit.*, Roll 2, p. 99.

10. Ibid., Roll 2, Tablets 9-17, p. 95.

11. Irwin to CIA, September 6, 1877, NSHS, MS 2723, Roll 721.

12. Letters Received, Office of Indian Affairs, Spotted Tail Agency, 1877, NSHS, MS 2723, Roll 841.

13. E.A. Brininstool, *Crazy Horse, The Invincible Oglala Sioux Chief* (Los Angeles: Wetzel Publishing Company, 1949), pp. 33, 45, 66.

14. Ricker, *loc. cit.*, Roll 2, p. 96. John G. Bourke, *On the Border with Crook* (New York: Charles Scribner's Sons, 1891), p. 422. Miller, *Ghost Dance*, p. 287. George E. Hyde, *Spotted Tail's Folk: A History of the Brulé Sioux* (Norman: University of Oklahoma Press, 1961), p. 253. Frederick Webb Hodge, *Handbook of American Indians North of Mexico*, Vol. 1 (Washington, D.C.: GPO, 1910), p. 359.

15. Eleanor H. Hinman, *Oglala Sources on the Life of Crazy Horse*, reprint from *Nebraska History* 57 (Spring 1976), pp. 20, 27-8.

Chapter 7

1. E.A. Brininstool, "How Chief Crazy Horse Died," *Nebraska History* 12 (January 1929): 22.

2. Joseph Epes Brown, *The Sacred Pipe* (Norman: University of Oklahoma Press, 1953), pp. 14-5.

Chapter 8

1. Lee to CIA, September 17, 1877, NSHS, MS 2723, Roll 841.

2. Ibid., September 8, 1877.

3. Ibid., October 31, 1877.

4. McCrary to Secretary of the Interior, April 3, 1877, NSHS, MS 2723, Roll 721.

5. E.A. Brininstool, "How Chief Crazy Horse Died," *Nebraska History* 12 (January 1929): pp. 54-56.

6. Eli S. Ricker, NSHS, MS 8, Roll 1.

7. Luther Standing Bear, *My People, The Sioux* (Boston: Houghton Mifflin Company, 1953), p. 100.

8. Susan Bordeaux Bettelyoun Manuscript, NSHS, MS 185, p. 8.

INDEX